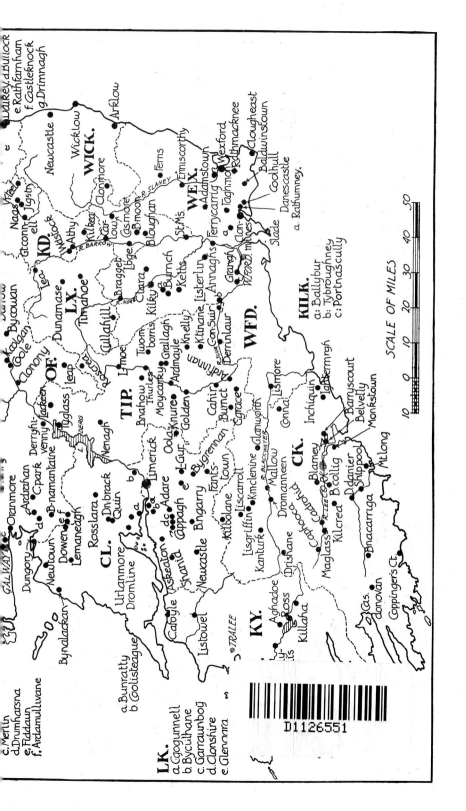

IRISH CASTLES

AND CASTELLATED HOUSES

RATHMACNEE CASTLE

IRISH CASTLES
AND CASTELLATED HOUSES

By
HAROLD G. LEASK
M. Arch., M.R.I.A.I., M.R.I.A.
Hon. F.S.A., Litt.D. (h.c.)
late President of the Royal Society of Antiquaries
of Ireland.
late Inspector of National Monuments in Eire.

1999
DUNDALGAN PRESS (W. TEMPEST) LTD.
DUNDALK

First Edition — December, 1941
Second Edition (*revised and added to*) — March, 1944
Reprinted revised — July, 1946 and August, 1951
Reprinted — March, 1964
Reprinted — September, 1973
Reprinted — September, 1977
Reprinted — April, 1986
Reprinted — July, 1995
Reprinted — May, 1999

Printed and Published at the
Dundalgan Press, Dundalk

ACKNOWLEDGMENTS.

While the greater part of the material in this book is the fruit of the author's own study and research, he gratefully acknowledges much assistance from more than one institution and person. In the first place, he owes the opportunities for seeing many hitherto unrecorded or inadequately studied castles to his official position in the service of the Commissioners of Public Works. The Commissioners have kindly permitted him to make use of the knowledge so gained and have also allowed him to utilise the official surveys of National Monuments in State care for some of the illustrations in this book. These surveys were, in many cases, made by the Clerks of Works employed in the service—Messrs. Gillooly, Dowdall, and O'Toole. To the Commissioners and their servants the author renders his most sincere thanks.

He is also indebted to the Council of the Royal Archæological Institute of Great Britain and Ireland for the use of the blocks of Trim and Limerick castles, the capitals at Athenry, and the plans of the keep at Carrickfergus—the last named having been made with the permission of the Minister of Finance of Northern Ireland.

Finally the author's thanks are due to the Council of the Royal Society of Antiquaries of Ireland for the loan of the illustrations of Clara, Nenagh, Shanid, Loughmoe, Taaffe's and Greencastle (Inishowen) Castles, Askeaton Hall and Knockgraffon mote; to the Irish Tourist Association for permission to use the illustrations of Castletowngeoghegan mote-and-bailey and King John's Castle, Carlingford, and to Messrs Thomas H. Mason & Sons for the views of Limerick and Cahir Castles; to the editor of the Journal of the Galway Archæological Historical Society for permission to re-publish the drawings of Derryhivenny castle; to the editor of the Ulster Journal of Archæology for the use of the blocks of Burt Castle; and to Mr. Henry H. Hill, A.R.I.B.A., of Cork, for the material from which the section of Blarney Castle has been prepared.

H.G.L.

ABBREVIATIONS

used in the illustrations.

Db	Drawbridge.
Dn or DN	Downwards (of stairs).
F	Chimney flue.
Fp	Fireplace.
G	Garderobe.
Ope.. ..	Opening.
Over.. ..	On storey above.
T	Timber trusses of roof.
Up or UP	Upwards (of stairs).
W	Window.

The figures 1, 2, 3, following indicate the floor referred to.

Meanings of the terms not explained in the text itself will be found in the glossary at page 163.

CONTENTS.

LIST OF PLATES.

The pen and ink drawings are all given in the index at the end of the book distinguished by their italic figure numbers.

INTRODUCTORY.

Spread over the Irish countryside there is a quite surprising number of ancient buildings, both large and small, whose strong walls, narrow loop-holes and meagre windows proclaim a military or at least defensive purpose. No traveller can fail to see them whilst all must feel some degree of curiosity about buildings which the maps declare to be castles. Many as are the easily seen remains, a sheet by sheet examination of the larger scale maps of the Ordnance Survey will reveal the existence—now or in the past—of still greater numbers.

What were these castles ? Fortresses of king or baron ; strong houses of lesser chieftains or later gentry ? The answers are not always easy to come by and when found are often inconclusive. It is indeed no simple task to search the journals of the learned societies, national or local, in which much information regarding Irish castles is to be found. Scattered throughout these publications are descriptions and historical notices of more or less notable examples. There are also lists of the extant and vanished castles of certain districts. But even for the professed antiquary the search is a laborious one, and he, after all his labour, cannot but observe how incomplete is our knowledge of this phase of Irish architecture.

While this is true of the buildings themselves the meagreness of historical references to them is even more notable. It is indeed strange that Irish buildings, lay or ecclesiastical, have received so little notice from annalist or historian ; how rare are the references to builders or buildings, no matter how important the latter may have been or still are. To arrive at even tentative conclusions as to the time of their erection the student of ancient Irish buildings is forced to rely to a very great extent upon the evidence of the structures themselves ; often it is only by a comparison of their features and details with those of better-dated buildings abroad that he can arrive at even approximate datings.

No comprehensive study of Irish castles, their history and architecture, has yet been made but some earnest workers have laid its foundations. More than a century ago Francis Grose, the antiquary, drew and caused to be engraved many sketches of the ecclesiastical and military remains of this country, while, in the middle of the last century, that splendid draughtsman, G. V. Du Noyer, added his more accurate contributions. Parker, student and publicist of English medieval architecture, read a paper upon Irish castles before the Society of Antiquaries of London. It was the fruit of a short visit to Ireland and, though partial, is quite excellent in its way. In more recent years several Irish antiquaries have worked in the field. Thomas Johnson Westropp, the most distinguished, scheduled the castles of Limerick and Clare and described many of them ; James Coleman and others compiled lengthy lists for Cork and Kerry, while Colonel Nolan studied, in some detail, the castles of the large barony of Clare in Galway. Lord Walter Fitzgerald, Canon Carrigan, and Philip Hore did much to record and describe those of Kildare and Leix, Ossory and Wexford. Dr. Goddard Orpen also did his share, especially in drawing attention to the earthen fortresses of the Anglo-Norman invaders ; many of these structures, in the then state of our knowledge, had been regarded as native works of prehistoric date.

A valuable book, entitled " The Ancient Castles of Ireland," written by Miss C. L. Adams, appeared in 1902. It is, avowedly, historical rather than critical in the architectural sense and, while admitting some castles that are not ancient, omits mention of over a score of important thirteenth century buildings. Engagingly written, it has a good historical bibliography.

Never quite abandoned, though relatively neglected, the study of Irish castles is still being advanced by several workers, and valuable contributions have been published recently in the Preliminary Survey of the Ancient Monuments of Northern Ireland.

There is one serious defect, however, in much of what has been done : a lack of adequate plans and other illustrations. These are essential to any critical analysis of the buildings, to the judgement of their evolution, growth, change and dating. Through them only can comparative studies be made. This lack is not hard to explain, and the antiquary must not be judged too harshly for his failure to supply it. In itself the labour of field work and research leaves insufficient time to survey and plan the buildings which are the object of his study. Moreover, the physical difficulties are great ; ruinous and encumbered with vegetation and debris, floorless and inaccessible as so many of the castles are, it is little wonder that few have been thoroughly surveyed. Mantles of the ubiquitous ivy, also, all too often make even a photograph impossible or of little value.

Nevertheless the defect is being overcome and there is now gathered material enough to justify the making of a book ; a general survey of six centuries of the military and semi-military architecture of Ireland. Final and definitive it cannot be—future research may upset some conclusions which now seem satisfactory enough—but that it will fill a gap and serve a purpose useful to both the student and the interested layman is the earnest hope of the author.

I

WHAT IS A CASTLE ?

The word castle has acquired a rather wide meaning. In its strictest application, the medieval one, it signifies a fortress of mortared stone erected by king or noble to guard a strategic position, or overawe a district, and serve as a residence for the owner or his deputy and retainers. But the term was also applied to the fortresses of earth, the mound or mote-and-bailey erections, thrown up by the Normans, not only in Normandy itself but in England and Ireland, at their first coming. The annalists tell us that such forceful figures as Hugh de Lacy built " castles " at many places throughout his fiefs. Later historians have been prone to accept the stone castles still extant at some of these places as original works of de Lacy. It is obvious, however, that in his short fighting career in Ireland Hugh had not the leisure or the means to embark upon building permanent structures of mortared stone. Indeed, he fell—at the hands of a young Irishman—into the fosse at Durrow (Offaly) around the mote there, while superintending the erection of this, the last of his works, which stands to this day.

Not only are these fortresses of earth—deeply fossed and crowned by palisades and towers of timber—the progenitors of the later stone erections, to be included in the term castle ; so also are the much later buildings, the well-defended tower-houses characteristic of the fifteenth and sixteenth centuries ; custom will have it so and custom is sufficiently justified by the military aspect of the buildings.

If the Anglo-Norman mote-and-bailey is a castle may
it not be said that the native Irish dún, cashel, great ring fort
or rath is equally worthy of the title ?   Hardly, it belongs to a
very different order of things and is the consequence of a
different outlook on life, of different manners and customs in
both war and peace, while the castle is essentially a product
of the feudal system in which the few might overawe and hold
the many in subjection.   Apart from such considerations the
study of the Irish defensive works—which is in an even less
advanced stage than that of the Irish medieval and later
castles—would take us back far into prehistory, beyond the
limits to which this book must be confined.

The annalists tell us, however, that the Irish built some
castles before the coming of the Normans. Seven are recorded :
Ballinasloe, Galway, Collooney, Athlone, Cuileanntrach, Tuam
and Ferns.   All were erected, demolished or burnt between
the years 1124 and 1166.   The evidence goes to show that they
were not castles of mortared stone.   Ballinasloe, the first,
built in 1124, was " burned by casual fire " in 1131.   That at
Galway was also erected in 1124 only to be burned and
demolished eight years later.   As for the castle of Athlone the
evidence that it was not a permanent erection of stone is
even more convincing.   The Annals of the Four Masters
record, under the date 1129 :—" The castle (Caislean) of
Athlone and the bridge were erected by Turlough O'Conor in
the summer of this year : the summer of the drought."   In
1131, say the Annals of Clonmacnoise, it " was burned by a
thunderbolt."   The inference that the castle of Athlone was
mainly one of timber seems inescapable.   Moreover, since the
object of O'Conor's castle and bridge was that he might take
the spoils of Meath at his pleasure, it is highly probable that
his fortress was on the Leinster bank of the river, a bridge-
head castle there which must not be confused with the existing
relic built by the Normans on the Connaught side for a similar
purpose against that province.   Tuam castle has disappeared
while that at Ferns, demolished in 1166, is certainly not
represented by the splendid and very Norman relic to be seen
there to-day.

It seems, then, that the Irish pre-Norman " castles " were not of the same character as the great structures raised wherever the invaders gained a secure foothold and that to-day there remains no vestige of a native Irish castle of the twelfth century.

The first military works of the Normans were little more than entrenched camps set up to serve a purely temporary purpose. Such, for instance were the earthworks at the headland of Baginbun, fitzStephen's camp in 1169 after the landing at Bannow. Later, Strongbow, Raymond le Gros and de Lacy and their vassals, spreading their conquests, raised " castles " throughout the newly acquired territories.

Strongbow's immense fief comprised the greater part of Leinster and its richest lands ; Hugh de Lacy's earldom of Meath, coterminous with the ancient kingdom, was almost as extensive and equally productive. To the north, John de Courcy, " Conquestor Ultoniæ," acquired by the might of his sword, an extensive demesne in Antrim and Down, while in English Uriel (Louth) others took and held rich lands. It is in these territories, which first came under the invaders' yoke, that by far the greater number of the earthen fortresses, the high motes with their baileys, is to be found. Not many years ago there was an important controversy between prominent antiquarians as to whether these mounds or motes were of Norman origin or were to be ascribed to earlier, native, builders. At that time the critical examination of the early military earthworks of Norman England had barely begun. Their study has since shown conclusively that the typical mote-and-bailey is a product of Norman military genius, and it is now clear that most of the similar works in Ireland must be ascribed to the invaders. It is equally certain that these soldiers remodelled for their own purposes some pre-existing earthworks which readily lent themselves to the process.

Some of these earthen fortresses have been described but so few have been surveyed that accurate plans and sections are not available. The field for survey is, indeed, still so much a virgin one that the early Norman " castle " of earth can be treated of here only in the most summary fashion.

B

The standard type, the mote-and-bailey, took its simplest form when erected upon a level site. It consisted of a high, flat-topped mound, the mote—encompassed by a deep fosse or ditch, adjoined to a larger entrenched area at a lower level—the base court or bailey. The fosses dug around both parts of this composite structure provided the material which was heaped up in the mound or mote itself and the bank or vallum of the bailey. The fosse of the mote was very deep since it had to supply the great mass of earth of which that high mound was built. The bailey fosse, which was connected—on one side at least—with the larger excavation, did not require to be so deep ; it had but to provide material for a comparatively low bank, and, sometimes, for the raised floor of the bailey itself. Both the mote and the vallum or bank encircling the bailey within its fosse, were crowned by palisades of heavy timber. On the summit of the mote was the house or wooden tower of the commander while within the bailey stood the quarters of his troops. Connecting the mote and bailey was a sloping wooden gangway or bridge. Close to the mote the bank and fosse of the bailey were usually omitted to give place for the entrance gate and, in some cases, it is also evident that the palisade of the bailey crossed the fosse and was carried up the slope of the mote so its top.

The sketch (Fig. 1) is of a mote-and-bailey in its most simple form. In it the bailey is of crescentic shape but other

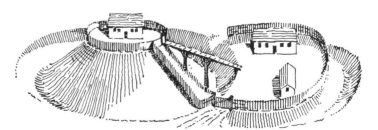

Re-construction of a Mote-and-Bailey.

Fig. 1.

Plate 1

CASTLETOWNGEOGHEGAN
MOTE-AND-BAILEY

KNOCKGRAFFON MOTE

plans were also adopted; square with rounded corners or D-shaped for instance. It will be seen that the high mote commanded the gateway and the greater part of the perimeter of the whole work, indeed every part of the bailey itself and its defences except that furthest away. Its own deep fosse made the mote highly defensible and provided a last refuge for the defenders should the bailey be captured. It could also become—like the quarter deck of the old sailing ship— the citadel of the commander and his faithful officers against the mutinous should the occasion arise.

Some of these strongholds show evidence of change and growth; the addition of another bailey for instance, or of a fore-work or barbican to the entrance. On sites which were not level the military works were cunningly adapted to the natural features. A boss or outcrop of rock served the purpose of a mote; a natural hillock—or perchance, a prehistoric tumulus—was remodelled or raised for the purpose. That the Norman, on occasion, made use of earlier Irish earthworks, altering them to his special purpose is only to be expected and several sites in Ireland and in Wales afford evidence of the practice. It was a not uncommon thing with him to adapt a low, narrow ridge, an esker or drumlin, for example, to the purpose of a fortress. By the excavation of a fosse across the ridge at a little distance from its higher end and there heaping up the soil so gained a mote was easily made. Similarly, the excavation of a trench along and across the ridge provided, with little labour, the banks and platform of the bailey.

While, in most instances the mote was part of the perimeter of the defences, in others it was sited within a fosse which encircled the whole fortress.

The late Dr. Goddard Orpen, historian of the Normans in Ireland, visited and described more than a score of their earthen works in Ossory, Westmeath and Louth. More than forty in Down and Antrim alone have been described by Mr. H. C. Lawlor, a close student and the best authority for that area. An analysis of these descriptions shows that the average height of the motes above the bottom of the encircling fosse was about 30 feet and the diameters of their level tops 60 feet. The baileys varied both in number, shape and size. Two or more are sometimes found, the crescent shape is common but U-, D-, or hatchet shapes also occur. while there are instances of the entire absence of the bailey. A small bailey might be but 70 feet across, an average one 125 feet in greatest dimension, while larger examples reach as much as 200 feet. In width, i.e., at right angles to the axis of mote and bailey, dimensions of 60 to 150 feet are found. The interior surface of the bailey is a platform, usually at a higher level than the ground outside its fosse.

But not all of the Norman earthworks were strictly of the mote-and-bailey type. Some had a lower and more spacious mound only slightly elevated above the adjoining bailey ; others were still simpler, merely palisaded entrenchments, often of rectangular plan. It is probable that the high motes, in some cases, and the lesser earthworks almost certainly, were provided with the famous wooden towers—the bretêsches. These structures, pre-fabricated timber block-houses, made to be readily taken apart for transport and as readily put together again, appeared on the Bayeux " Tapestry "—which is really an embroidery, not a tapestry—(p. 162), and are mentioned in the literature of the invasion. Brattice and bratticing, denoting temporary wooden galleries or hourds (p. 17) and also bartizan (p. 19) derive from the old French breteche. The Irish place-name Brittas is believed to be derived, in some cases, from this very bretêsche.

There are many high and mote-like mounds in almost every part of Ireland but not all of them are Norman. Some, perhaps most, are tumuli covering prehistoric burials but this class of monument is seldom flat-topped. The absence of any sign of an attached bailey is not always a proof of an Irish origin ; the bailey may have been removed by cultivation. Even where this has happened, however, there sometimes remains some barely visible indication of the old banks and ditches. The presence of *concentric* banks and ditches, on the other hand, is almost conclusive proof of a non-Norman origin for the earthwork ; this seems to be a definitely Irish form.

When first erected the new mote would not provide a secure foundation for a heavy structure of stone ; many years had to elapse before the earth was sufficiently consolidated. It is certain, none the less, that some motes were crowned with stone towers. Where the core of the mote was a natural hillock, this naturally gave solid support for heavy stone erections and at least one stone keep, founded on a mote of this kind remains. It is at Shanid, Co. Limerick (Plate II and Fig. 2) and will be described later.

To what period are these mote-and-bailey " castles " to be ascribed ? When did mote building give place to the erection of castles of stone ? The evidence adduced by historians, notably Dr. Orpen, is that most of the earth fortresses must belong to the years between the coming of Strongbow and his followers, and the close of the twelfth century ; that of the military occupation of the newly acquired fiefs, the early years of the invasion and the expansion of the adventurers' power. This seems the most reasonable, indeed obvious conclusion.

Not until the invaders had acquired greater security and had perfected their organization could they begin the building of the great stone castles. It is not to the first generation of the Normans, Strongbow, Le Gros, de Lacy and the like, that we owe the fully developed castle, but to their successors and to the royal authority that sought to curb them.

Shanid

Fig. 2.

II

ITS DEFENCE AND ITS PARTS.

The whole field and development of the military arts of attack and defence is so large a subject as to require a treatise to itself; it must be treated here in rather summary fashion.

Attacker and defender alike used the small arms of the times; the short bow, the famous longbow, and the more lethal arbalest or crossbow. While the first was the earliest form the cross-bow was certainly in use in the twelfth century and continued as a weapon for quite four hundred years. The long bow—typical weapon of the English armies in the French wars—was very effective in open battle or from the alures of a castle but was not so suitable for use in the relatively confined wall embrasures of the fortress. Its very length was a disadvantage here but the smaller span of the steel bow of the arbalest—about 30 inches—made it an ideal weapon for the defender; he could discharge it readily from positions quite close up to the loop hole of his embrasure. Of course, its rate of fire was slow in comparison with that of the longbow, a great disadvantage in the open but less so to the bowman under cover. Its range and penetrating power were greater than those of the long bow. The setting of so powerful a weapon required considerable force, more than even a strong man could apply without some extraneous aid, and one of the simplest equipments and methods is shown in Fig. 3. Holding his bow upside down—or rather inside out—the bowman inserts his foot in the stirrup at the end of the bow, and catches the cord with a metal hook depending from a

A Crossbowman setting his bow
(after Viollet-le-Duc)

Fig. 3.

strong belt worn about his waist. Strong pressure downwards with the foot bends the bow and pulls the cord back till it engages in a metal catch, connected with and ready to be released by the long trigger shown in the illustration. This operation completed, the missile—a bolt—would be placed in its groove on the upper side of the wooden stock from whence it would be propelled on the actuation of the trigger. The bolts or quarrels were heavy, un-notched arrows of wood, about sixteen inches long, and having metal points. They were winged, not with feathers, but with thin strips of wood or leather ; sometimes skin or horn was used for the same purpose. One form of quarrel had a broad, square head, with raised points, designed to give a smashing blow to armour. So much for the minor weapons of offence and defence.

The main function and justification of a defensive work, be it of earth, wood or stone, is to enable relatively few defenders to withstand with success the attacks of greater numbers. The early palisaded motes and baileys could not fulfil this function perfectly ; not only were the timber palisades vulnerable to fire—perhaps their greatest danger— but they could be torn down in a concentrated attack, while a large garrison was needed to man their whole extent. It is not surprising, therefore, that they gave place to uninflammable and compact stone walls. The attackers could no

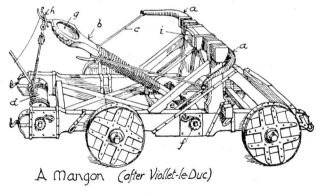

A Mangon (after Viollet-le-Duc)

Fig. 4.

longer hope to set such defences on fire or tear them down easily ; he was forced to adopt the slower tactics of battery or mining. His engines for casting or slinging heavy missiles against or over the walls—first the mangon and later the trebuchet—were designed for these purposes.

There were many forms of the stone casting machine called the mangon but the principle of all was the same. The mangon shown (Fig. 4) is one of the more complicated. In essentials, the machine consisted of a combination of a heavy bow, " a," which operated a moving beam, " b," called the " bride." This, with the cord of the bow hooked over it, was drawn back by the windlass " d " into a horizontal position and additional tension was given to it by winding up the twisted cords " e " at its axle by means of the cogged wheel and ratchets at " f." The missile—a rounded stone—was placed in the spoon-like bowl " g " at the end of the bride. On the release of the trigger " h " the bride sprang upwards violently and, striking the padded framework at " i " with great force, cast its missile forwards. The wheels of the framework were detachable and only used in the moving of the engine from place to place.

The trebuchet (Fig. 5) was a much larger machine designed to cast heavy stones on a relatively high trajectory to a great distance against or over the walls of a fortress or town. Its long beam, " a,"— nicknamed the " verge "— turned upon a horizontal axle in an upright and strongly braced wooden frame. At one end of the verge there hung a box, " c," filled with stones or earth. This rose as the verge was drawn down into the position " x," by means of the hand windlasses shown, and the sling, " b," was loaded with a missile and laid in position in the trough, " d." Released by a trigger contrivance, the verge flew upwards to " y," and the sling whirled through the air until—checked by the cord, " e "—it suddenly released its missile. Modifications in the length of " e " altered the trajectory and range of the missile.

Mangon and trebuchet were the cannon of pre-gunpowder days and were essentially battering engines, though the latter,

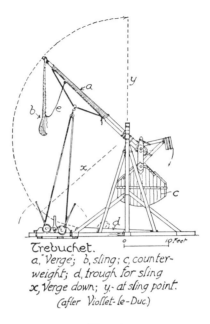

Trebuchet.
a, Verge; b, sling; c, counter-
weight; d, trough for sling
x, Verge down; y, at sling point.
(after Viollet-le-Duc.)

Fig. 5.

at times, used rather strange ammunition—even dead animals were hurled into the midst of the enemy. Such heavy and violently vibrating machines were ill-suited for mounting upon walls and towers ; they could shake them to pieces and it is probable that the larger engines, at least, were used only by the attackers.

As the angle of fire was raised to throw the missiles over the walls into the interior space, the defender had to raise his walls to greater heights. But when he had done so another defect in his defences became apparent : he was no longer able to see from the wall tops what was happening at their bases. Here the miners, safe in the " dead-ground " out of view, might be at work sapping the foundations in order that the wall might fall and a breach be made for the entry of the attackers. The defenders could only obtain a view of the ground close to the walls, or fire upon the miners, by leaning out through the crenellations of the wall top. In such a posture the bowman in the castle was exposed to the archers of his foe. To afford the necessary protection the hourd or hoarding was developed. This was a timber gallery (Fig. 6) at the level of the wall-walk, supported on beams passing through the walls, and usually roofed in and faced with timber. In its floor were openings through which missiles could be dropped directly on the attackers below, while, to afford protection against flaming darts, the woodwork was sometimes covered with fresh ox-hides. In time the hoarding gave place to a permanent projecting structure of stone, a parapet borne upon corbels or brackets between which were the downward-looking openings— the machicolations (Fig. 7)—without which no picture of a medieval castle seems quite convincing.

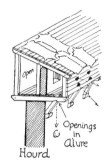

Fig. 6.

The timber hoardings seem in Ireland—to judge by the number of castles which have no flanking towers to their outer walls—to ante-date the introduction of this later, and rather obvious method of defence, well known at a much earlier period in the East, where it was used by Turk and Crusader alike. Such towers, projecting outwards from the castle walls, enabled the defenders to see and command the ground between them by flanking fire. Moreover, when the towers were carried to a greater height than the walls themselves, they commanded the wall-tops upon which the enemy might—by means of scaling ladders or assault towers—have secured a footing.

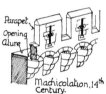

In some early castles the flanking towers were square in plan. This shape was defensively weak for two reasons : the square angles were easily broken down and the straight face of the tower was scarcely more defensible than a similar length of the ordinary curtain wall. The weakness was recognized early and the nearly round or D-shaped tower came into being. That this shape is much stronger against assault by battery is obvious and that it eliminated " dead ground " at the tower's base is hardly less so. Curtain walls provided with many towers, spaced not too far apart, were formidable defences which enabled the small garrisons, concentrated in

Fig. 7.

the towers rather than spread along the walls, to command very effectively all parts of the fortress and the " field " around it.

Most castles were, of course, further protected by a ditch, a fosse or moat, usually filled with water. To approach the walls closely the attackers, whether miners or assault troops, had to fill in at least some part of the fosse, usually with faggots or earth. This was a lengthy job since it could only be carried out in piecemeal fashion by workmen protected in various ways, by movable sheds, for instance, pushed slowly forward towards the walls as the filling proceeded. Safe within the sheds, when contact with the walls had been made, the miners could carry on their burrowing. Upon the filled-in causeway too, mighty assault towers of wood could be moved forward until close against the walls themselves and from the summits of the moving towers the attackers could reach the wall-tops. Whether any of these great engines of warfare ever figured in the siege of an Irish castle we cannot tell.

Broadly and briefly speaking, the palisade gave place to the stone wall—often erected on the same lines or " trace "—and to the wall there were added flanking towers—a later development which formed an integral part of the later castles from their foundation. Naturally these towers were more needed at the angles of the fortress, where they commanded the adjacent lengths of the curtains and a wide area of the " field," but, where the curtains were of considerable length, intermediate towers were required and, usually, provided. These might be single towers or parts of a gate-building, as at Dundrum, Roscommon, Dublin, Limerick and other castles to be mentioned in their turn. In such cases the towers of the gate structure flanked the main entrance which was between them, with narrow loops commanding the space in front of the gate.

So much for the walls and towers ; their parts and the other features and the technical terms by which they are known next claim attention. It will be convenient to devote a paragraph to each of the more important.

The features which first catch the eye—without which, indeed, we can hardly recognise a castle to be a castle at all—are its battlements with their crenellations (from *Low Latin : Crena*, a notch) ; the thin parapet walls which sheltered the defenders of the wall tops, notched at regular intervals by narrow openings (Fig. 7a). The solid short lengths of parapet between the notches are known as merlons, a French word derived from the Latin *murus*. These are often pierced centrally by a narrow loop-hole for the bowman. The parapets and crenellations, being relatively slight in construction, were easily destroyed and in many of the Irish castles they have disappeared. What was called the " slighting " of a castle in Cromwellian times meant making it indefensible—throwing down its parapets and breaching its walls. Much similar " slighting " has been done, through pure mischief, in our own day ; it is so easy to overthrow a weather-worn parapet.

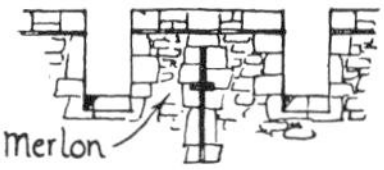

merlon

Crenellations. 13th Cy.

Fig. 7a.

Behind the parapet was the alure or wall-walk, of the full thickness of the wall less that of the parapet. It was sometimes made wider—by the addition of plank flooring carried upon corbels or brackets projecting from the inner face of the wall. The term alure is also applied to the planked walk within the hourd, but outside the wall, which has already been described.

The place of this perishable timber erection was taken, in the castles of the fourteenth and later centuries, by permanent stonework, the parapet being placed in front of the main wall-face, and borne by lintels or arches resting upon corbels. Between these were the openings, looking downwards, from which the defenders could drop missiles or shoot down upon the attackers below. Unfortunately few continuous machicolations—the name of this form of structure—remain on any Irish castle wall top. Short projecting features of the kind, *machicoulis* (Fig. 8), generally placed to command an entrance or an exposed angle, are to be found, however, in our castles of both late and early dates. The angular variety has come to be known as a bartizan, a word given great vogue by Sir Walter Scott, and deriving from bratticing. (p. 10).

Machicoulis

'Bartizan'.

from Donore

Fig. 8.

The base part of most castle walls usually projects, splaying boldly outwards. This talus- or base-batter not only added solidity and stability to the wall but it served another, a military, purpose ; it caused stones or other missiles, dropped through the openings of hourd or machicolation, to rebound outwards upon the assailants.

Embrasure

Fig. 9.

Loop:
Roscommon

Fig. 10.

Openings in the outer walls were, for obvious reasons, of narrow width towards the outside. Even where their only purpose was to admit light and air they were splayed to a greater width towards the inside. Many of these loops, as they are called, which remain in our ruined fortresses to-day, tall perhaps but only a few inches in width, can have had so limited a field of observation or fire, even though splayed widely inwards, that they cannot have served a defensive purpose. Loops of the kind are most usually found at the lower levels in the walls. The real defensive loop is different ; it is pierced through the thinner stonework of a wide, and often almost square, inner embrasure : a niche, a small room in itself (Fig. 9). Within this embrasure the bowman had plenty of freedom of movement to right or left, to discharge his bolt sideways. He thus commanded with his eye and weapon quite a large area of the outer ground. The loop also descended below the floor of the niche, to permit of shooting downwards, and was often provided also with notches at its sides, about breast height, to increase the field of fire to the right or left. The result is the cross form of loop-hole (Fig. 10). This was further developed, after the middle of the thirteenth century, by circular expansions of the opening at its extremities, the arms, head, and base of the cross ; giving the form to be found at Ferns, Clonmore and Ballymoon castles (Fig. 11), repeated *ad nauseam* in the pseudo " castles " of the nineteenth century. In castles erected after the advent of firearms many, though not all, of the loops are even simpler in form : mere circular holes of small size or similar expansions of plain upright loops.

Loop:
Clonmore

Fig. 11.

The entrance gateways of most castles could be isolated at will from the outer ground by draw-bridges of timber.

These were of four different types. The simplest and probably the earliest kind was truly a " draw " bridge—a horizontal timber platform which could be drawn in and out, working upon rollers. A later and—pictorially—more familiar type was a platform, hinged at its inner end and raised by chains attached to its outer corners ; the chains passed through slots in the wall to a windlass within. There was another and much more complicated type, also in use—though perhaps not in Ireland—consisting of two parts connected to work together : the hinged bridge, outside the gateway, and a heavy strong door working on a horizontal axle near its top, within the gate. The sides or stiles of the door frame were very long, projecting upwards like two horns, and when the bridge was in the " down " position the door was also horizontal but near the ceiling of the gate passage, its horns or arms jutting out over the bridge. Chains connected the ends of the horns with the bridge and—as the door was lowered—the bridge rose against the wall. The gateway was thus doubly closed. Very tall wall-slots were, of course, required for the arms of horns of the door, features which have not, so far, been recognized in any Irish castle. The fourth type of drawbridge (which the French call *pont-a-bascule*) was a level or slightly tilted platform, with an axle in the centre of its length, rising and falling in the manner of a see-saw. It was only used within the walls of the passage through the gate or barbican. The bridges in the west gate of Roscommon castle and the south gate at Trim may have been of this type but the nature of the mechanical contrivances by which they were operated at these places can only be guessed at. For this reason a conjectural restoration is not attempted here.

The term barbican is often misunderstood and requires some explanation. It is a fore-work, situated in advance of the gateway tower or gate. Usually, as at Trim (Fig. 12), it stood on the outer edge of the fosse or moat. A splendid example, the finest in Ireland, is St. Lawrence's Gate at Drogheda, protecting the real gate, now quite destroyed, which stood in the town walls *within* the moat. Between gateway and barbican there was usually a draw-bridge.

Trim:
Barbican
Fig. 12.

Groove

Portcullis.

Fig. 13.

But the draw-bridge was only part of the protection of the castle gate ; within it was the portcullis—a heavy framework of timber, shod, bolted and strapped with iron (Fig. 13), which could be raised or lowered in the grooves in the stonework still often to be seen. The windlass for operating the portcullis was in a room over the gate passage ; the heavy framework could be raised through a wide slot in the floor of this room.

Within the portcullis were one or more heavy gates closing the entrance passage and secured by heavy crossbeams or bolts of timber. The square holes in the masonry into which the bolts could slide are often to be seen in the side walls ; they are often the only clues remaining to the position and previous existence of a gate.

The great towers of the early castles, the keeps, will be described when we come to the study of actual examples later but some more general remarks may find a place here. The term " keep " is the most usual but it is not the only one by which these towers are known. Donjon, whence " dungeon " from the use of some part of them as prisons—is one ; " Juliet " is another, but this is the special name for the cylindrical type of keep found in some early castles. Nenagh is the finest Irish example. In England two types of keep have been differentiated, the " hall " and " tower " types. The hall keep is oblong in plan and is believed to derive from the hall dwelling which goes back to Saxon times : a hall with an adjoining chamber or " solar," both raised upon a vaulted basement storey devoted to stores and cellarage. In the keep of the hall type the division of the main storey into two parts is not obvious externally, for the reason that the walls were carried up high above the roof on all sides. In the tower keeps, on the other hand, the chamber was in the storey over the hall and the whole building was, usually, more square in plan. This typology, however, is not generally accepted.

We cannot say that the Irish keeps followed either plan exactly. Possibly some of the more oblong examples, such as Athenry, Greencastle (Down), Lea, or Rinnduin were divided internally into hall and chamber. At Carrickfergus the hall was in the third storey, and at Trim, which is square internally, the hall and chamber are adjoined on the main floor ; at Maynooth, which is nearly square, they may also have been placed side by side. The cylindrical keeps, like those of Dundrum and Nenagh were, of course, of the tower type.

In one thing all the keeps agree—the main entrance doorway was on the level of the first floor above the ground. The approach to the doorway was, of necessity, by a flight of steps and most of the doorways must have been protected by a small structure of stone, known as a fore-building. Interesting fore-buildings remain in many English examples, but in the Irish castles this feature and the steps have disappeared. leaving little or no trace of their previous existence. It is, indeed, uncertain in many cases whether there were ever fore-buildings of stone ; timber may have been used in these structures.

Mural passages and chambers are common features of all castles. Some had a defensive purpose, some were perhaps sleeping rooms, others certainly garderobes or latrines, with their shafts discharging externally.

Valuable, though not always quite definite, criteria for the dating of castles and other medieval buildings are the shapes of the arches to doorways, windows and other openings (Fig. 14). The semicircular or half-round arch, usually associated with the Romanesque of the twelfth and earlier centuries, calls for no special description. This form was in use at all dates but when built in wrought sandstone and boldly moulded, as in the keep at Trim, it is a sure indication in castles, of a date round about 1200. Rough barrel vaulting, however. is no criterion of date whatever; it was in use over an extended period. Another form common about the end of the twelfth century, and also found at Trim, is the segmental arch, i.e., consisting of a segment only of a circle. Somewhat later, usually, is the pointed arch which, in its blunt form, is often found. Unfortunately for the student this arch persists

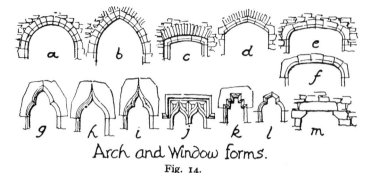

Arch and Window forms.

Fig. 14.

(a) Round or semicircular (Trim).

(b) Pointed (many castles and all dates).

(c) Segmental (Trim).

(d) Segmental pointed (Ballymoon).

(e) Four-centred (Donegal, fireplaces).

(f) Semi-elliptical (Kanturk, Mallow, Carrick).

(g) Trefoil-pointed (Athenry, Ferns, Lea).

(h) Ogee and (i) Cusped ogee (many XVth and XVIth century examples).

(j) Pair of ogee-headed lights with square hood-moulding.

(k and l) XVth century stepped and shouldered forms (Askeaton).

(m) the "Caernarvon" arch (early XIV century, Ballymoon and Ballyloughan).

in company with the round arch and in doorways especially, right up to the seventeenth century and its form, considered alone, is not much use as a dating feature.

The segmental-pointed arch, consisting of two segments of a circle, also occurs, and in castles indicates a date in the thirteenth or the fourteenth century. Several Irish examples seem to belong to *circa* 1250-1300. A beautiful mid- and late thirteenth century form of arch is the trefoil-pointed, found in windows at Ferns, Lea and Athenry.

What has been called the " Cærnarvon " arch—from its frequent occurrence in that splendid Welsh castle—is not an arch at all, but a combination of a lintel with two corbels. It is ascribable in Ireland to *circa* 1300 and the early part of the fourteenth century.

Thesemi- elliptical or three-centred arch (f) hardly requires description ; it seems, like the four-centred Tudor arch, to belong to the sixteenth and seventeenth centuries in Ireland.

III

THE MILITARY CASTLES OF STONE.

The earthen fortresses, the motes and baileys and lesser works, were ill-suited to be permanent residences however well they might serve in the early stages of the conquest. As in Normandy and Britain, they were in Ireland also, fated inevitably, to be abandoned for permanent structures of stone, more defensible and spacious and more comfortable to dwell in than their predecessors. Comfortless though the castles may now appear to us, their massive walls were a better defense not only against the assailant, but against the weather, than the little block-houses perched high upon the motes, or the other wooden buildings within the palisaded baileys.

The great castle building period in Ireland extended from the end of the twelfth century for about 130 years ; broadly speaking, from 1180 to 1310. In it were raised all the larger truly military castles which dominated the country until the advent of siege ordnance. Throughout the fourteenth century and the first half of the following hundred years we hear of no castle building though the records of repairs and re-edification are fairly numerous. The fourteenth century, indeed, was a period of little building activity, on the part of either church-man or layman in Ireland. Architecture in this country in this period, in contrast to that of England of the time, has little of interest to show. Some at least of the historical causes seem obvious. The invasion by Edward Bruce brought disorder and famine in its train while the great plague, the Black Death of 1349, cannot but have reduced the country to a still lower state of poverty from which recovery was slow. Whatever may have been the state of the people, high or low, the existing castles, despite vicissitudes, seemed to have continued to serve their primary purposes.

Most of the stone castles erected in Ireland, excepting those in the larger cities, up to about the middle of the thirteenth century have, as their dominating feature, a great tower, a " donjon," commonly called a keep. This tower is, indeed, the successor of the mote as are the courtyards or wards—enclosed by the curtain walls—successors to the palisaded baileys. Keeps are sometimes, though not often, erected upon or enclosing motes or in place of them. The stone curtains also, in some instances, follow the lines of older palisades of timber.

Though some few of the earlier castles are keepless it is with the keep-castles, typical of the first period, that we are now concerned. In these the great towers are of several different shapes or plans : rectangular, either square or oblong ; round or polygonal and of another form, which seems to be peculiar to Ireland, a rectangle furnished at each of its corners with a bold tower or turret.

While in some castles the keep forms part of the outer defences, in others it is isolated within the curtain walls, and it will be convenient, in this study, to group the castles according to the form of the keep and its place in the fortress. Such a grouping is typological but not chronological, since all the types were contemporary or nearly so.

The first group is that of the castles with keeps of rectangular plan which are either incorporated in the outer defences or stand isolated within the walls. Carrickfergus, Rinnduin and Greencastle (Donegal) belong to the first category of the group, and Trim, Adare, Maynooth, Athenry and Greencastle (Down) to the second.

The second main group is that which comprises the castles with round or polygonal keeps, in the same two categories—defined by the inclusion of the keep with the outer walls or its isolation within them. At Nenagh, and in the destroyed castle of Castleknock, the keep was part of the outer defences, while at Dundrum (Down), Shanid and Athlone it stands within the fortified area.

In the third group are all the castles with towered keeps, what may be called the specially Irish type. To it belong Carlow, Ferns, Lea and Terryglass, besides the vanished castle of Wexford and the reconstructed castle at Enniscorthy.

It will not be possible in these pages to discuss each individual castle in the above groups in full detail ; this has, indeed, already been done elsewhere,[1] but representative or specially notable structures will be dealt with, leaving to later chapters the discussion of castles which do not conform to the three main types.

CASTLES WITH RECTANGULAR KEEPS.

The most important of the castles belonging to the first main group is CARRICKFERGUS (Co. Antrim). The massive pile (Fig. 15) which still stands on the shores of Belfast Lough, was apparently the first real castle to be built in Ireland. One

Carrickfergus from the S. W.

Fig. 15.

[1] Leask : *Irish Castles : 1180 to 1310.* Jour. Royal Archæological Association of Great Britain & Ireland, vol. XCIII, pp. 143-199.

of the largest, it is also one of the few Irish examples on the continental or British scale. It was erected at some time between 1180 and *circa* 1205—the precise date is not known—either by John de Courcy, " Conquestor Ultoniæ," first of the Anglo-Norman invaders of Ulster, or by Earl Hugo de Lacy, the younger, who succeeded him in 1205. Because some of the details of the great keep—pairs of round-headed window lights beneath a round arch (Fig. 16)—are certainly of a type well-known in the twelfth century, it seems probable that de Courcy, rather than de Lacy, was the builder and at a date more probably before than after 1200.

Carrickfergus

Fig. 16

The site of the fortress is an irregular peninsula of rock isolated at the narrow—landward—end by an artificial ditch or fosse. At this end is the double-towered entrance building of the thirteenth century, altered at several succeeding periods. Two courtyards or wards, surrounded by curtain walls, occupy the whole of the peninsula, following its outline. The outer ward is of large size and very irregular in plan, while the inner ward is both smaller and rather more symmetrical. In its northern corner, abutting on the western curtain and the wall which divides the wards and thus commanding both of them—besides a considerable length of curtain—is the very massive keep (Plan, Fig. 17). It is so remarkable as to deserve a special and detailed description. Some 90 feet in height, it is nearly square in plan, measuring 58 feet by 56 feet, and its longer walls are from 9 to 12 feet in thickness. In it there were originally four storeys of which the topmost was raised at some time either to gain greater height or to obtain a fifth storey. The lowest of the storeys, which in the original building was approached only from above, consists of two long, vaulted rooms separated by a thick wall. In one of these rooms was, and is, the castle well, while from the same apartment rises the principal staircase, a vice or winding stairs, leading to all the upper storeys and the roof.

As in the majority of keeps the only entrance is at a storey height above the ground. It is round-headed and was provided with two sets of doors, but the fore-building, the

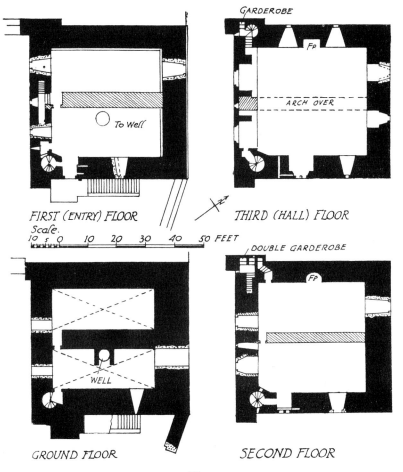

FIRST (ENTRY) FLOOR

Scale.

THIRD (HALL) FLOOR

GARDEROBE

Fp

ARCH OVER

To Well

GROUND FLOOR

WELL

SECOND FLOOR

DOUBLE GARDEROBE

Fp

Fig. 17.

Carrickfergus Keep, plan.

Trim Castle from the South East

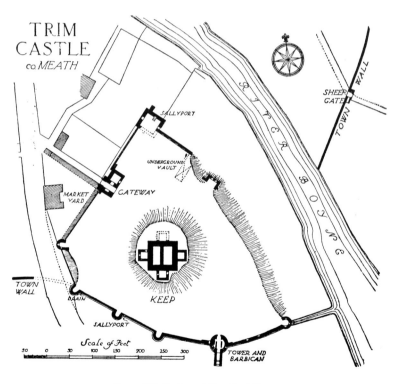

TRIM CASTLE
co. MEATH

SALLYPORT

UNDERGROUND VAULT

MARKET YARD

GATEWAY

RIVER BOYNE

SHEER GATE

TOWN WALL

TOWN WALL

DRAIN

SALLYPORT

KEEP

TOWER AND BARBICAN

Scale of Feet

50 0 50 100 150 200 250 300

From *Irish Castles and Castellated Houses*

small defensible structure which protected it—a usual feature of the castles of the period—has been removed. This storey and the next, the second floor, are also divided into two rooms by central walls but on the third floor is a single large apartment, the Great Hall of the castle. Its windows are relatively large in comparison to the mere loops which gave light, originally, to the storeys below. Three of the hall windows have paired round-headed lights set in deep embrasures similarly arched within and without. (Fig. 16). There is a large fireplace and the now lofty room is spanned by a great arch which bears the present roof. The original room was certainly lower and may have been divided into two halves by a row of timber posts. The south wall of the keep, as the least exposed to attack, contains the largest windows and a mural stairway which, at the south-western corner, gives access to the garderobes accommodated in a small tower or turret. This, like the stairs turret and two others at the opposite angles, is carried up above the level of the battlements. While lacking the broad and shallow external pilasters which are a feature of many Norman keeps in England, the Carrickfergus tower, in its rude massiveness, is not less impressive than these masterpieces of military art.

There are two other castles in this group, both later in date than Carrickfergus, which can only receive passing notice. Neither has as yet been studied in detail, the first because it is so heavily obscured by ivy and the second by reason of its much ruined condition. They are Rinnduin or Rindown[1] (Co. Roscommon), which is also a peninsular castle and has a rectangular keep incorporated in the curtain walls, and Greencastle[2] (Co. Donegal) where the keep similarly situated, is square in plan.

First among the castles with isolated rectangular keeps stands TRIM (Co. Meath), the largest Anglo-Norman fortress in Ireland (Fig. 18). Over three acres are enclosed within its walls which had a perimeter of some 1,500 feet. About the

[1] Fitzpatrick : Jour. R.S.A.I., vol. LXV, pp. 176-180.
[2] Ulster Jour. Arch. vol. XVI, pp. 10 ff.

year 1172 Hugh de Lacy, first of the name, raised a mote-and-bailey castle at Trim which was burned in the following year. Of its rebuilding there is no record. From the structural evidence provided by the keep—which replaced and apparently encloses some of the original mote—this remarkable building was erected about 1190-1200.

In plan (Fig. 19) the keep is unique ; it is square with a smaller square tower projecting from each of its sides. Each side measures about 65 feet in length and its greatest height— measured to the top of the highest corner turret—is over 76 feet. The lesser towers which remain project outwards 22 feet from the main structure. The eastern tower served as a fore-building and also housed the castle chapel on an upper floor, an arrangement found in some English castles, but on a larger scale. The walls of this and the other towers are relatively thin in comparison with those of the main building which are over 11 feet in thickness. These are pierced by the wide and lofty, round-headed embrasures (Fig. 20) of the not very numerous windows and the segmental-arched opening (Fig. 14c) of the principal doorway. In the thickness of these walls are the passages and stairways which are the means of access to the lesser towers and from floor to floor.

Trim

Fig. 20.

Externally the building is plain and unadorned, in limestone roughly coursed, sparingly punctuated by the very narrow original loops or the ragged holes which mark where once there were windows. Near the top the main wall-faces are set back a little but the corner turrets and the smaller towers rise sheerly upwards. Inside the building there were three lofty storeys, only the lower two being roofed in and divided by a heavy central wall. The larger of the two lowest rooms was probably the Hall, the smaller, which has a fireplace and numerous cupboards, the Chamber. Keeps of this plan are not uncommon in Norman England and have been called (not without some criticism) " Hall " keeps to distinguish them from the other common type, the " Tower " keep, in which the Chamber occupied the storey over the Hall.

Though the window and door openings, in their external aspects, have been changed or mutilated, in the interior they

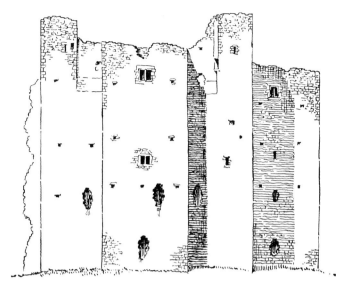

WEST ELEVATION

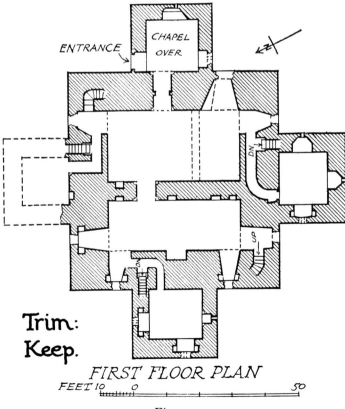

ENTRANCE

CHAPEL OVER

N

DN

UP

DN

Trim: Keep.

FIRST FLOOR PLAN

FEET 10   0   50

Fig. 19

Trim
Window

are still little altered. The main doorways have segmental heads and the round-arched window embrasures have bold mouldings in wrought sandstone. Both forms are character-istic of the period, as is the use of sandstone. In all Irish buildings this free-working stone was in use from the twelfth to the middle of the thirteenth century for all the wrought work about windows and doors, for pillars and their capitals and bases ; it was not until about 1260 that the abundant native limestone came into use for these purposes though it had long served as the ordinary material of plain walls.

The curtain walls of Trim, with the five remaining towers and one of the two gate-towers of the castle, are somewhat later than the keep. They appear to belong to about 1220, the year in which ". . . . the castle of Trim was built by William Peppard, Lord of Tabor." One of the gate towers, the South or Dublin gate—which is probably a little later in date—is remarkable, indeed unique in Ireland. It consists of a main tower, nearly round in plan, placed astride the curtain wall and pierced by the entrance passage-way. This is continued outwards between two crenellated walls to a bar-bican on the outer edge of the moat or fosse. There was a counter-balance drawbridge which, when raised, cut off the inner gate from the entrance in the barbican, which was commanded by the defenders from above. This gate-tower was the residence for a time of the boy, Prince Hal, later King Henry V, left here by Richard II in 1399, on his hasty return to England which was to end in defeat and death.

Though there are no historical references to a castle at ADARE prior to 1226, parts of the buildings there are of an earlier date (Fig. 21). The half-destroyed keep is square in plan (40 feet by 40 feet) and has slight but broad, pilaster like projections on two of its faces. It does not form part of the outer defences, but is incorporated in the curtain wall of the inner ward, which approximates to a circle in plan and appears to have been sited on an Irish ring-fort. The castle builders deepened the fosse around the fort, connecting it with the nearby river. The fosse still remains, in part,

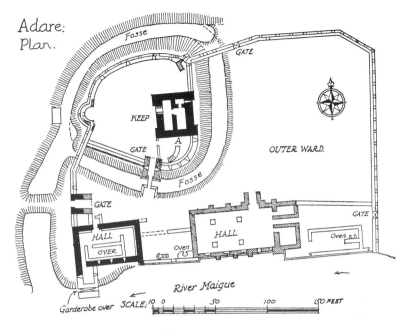

Fig. 21.

isolating the inner ward from the much larger outer ward, lying to the east and south and and extending to the banks of the River Maigue. Within this courtyard, and overlooking the river, are two hall buildings. That nearest the main gateway, which is on the west, is the more ancient of the two and is of two storeys in height. The lower storey is divided into several rooms, possibly stores or cellarage, but the upper part is entirely occupied by one apartment—the great Hall of the castle. Some of the original windows (Fig. 22) which remain—round-headed lights in pairs, bordered by heavy roll mouldings in sandstone—indicate a date about 1200. They are very similar to the west windows of the church of Manister or Monasternenagh, the large Cistercian abbey some miles away, which can be ascribed to the same date. Further eastwards is another hall which apparently took the place of the first hall in the thirteenth century. It was somewhat like

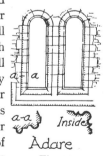

Adare
Fig. 22.

a church in having a porch and two aisles, and has the usual
buttery and traces of a kitchen at the eastern end. The
windows of this hall, pointed lights in pairs, overlook the
waters of the Maigue which lap the walls below.

It is no longer possible to see the full extent of the great
castle of the Fitzgeralds at MAYNOOTH (Co. Kildare), but a
fine gate-tower and a very massive keep remain to testify to
its former glory. The keep, isolated and probably of the
thirteenth century, is rectangular, lying north and south and
measuring 72 feet in this direction. It is 62 feet wide and has
walls 6½ feet in thickness about its two lofty storeys. Unfortunately there has been loss through destruction, and modern
restorations have so masked original features that an analysis
is difficult. There was a vaulted fore-building to the entrance
which is high up, 20 feet over ground level, in the eastern side
wall. This doorway leads directly into an apartment 55 feet
in length and of the full width of the building. Seemingly it
was originally divided into two halves by a timber partition
with a central stone pillar. The lower part of the keep was
also divided into two long rooms, but by a heavy central wall
carrying stone vaults. In two respects this structure is
peculiar—the central portions of three of its faces project
slightly, marking the positions of small wall chambers; and
there is a continuous vaulted mural gallery in the upper parts
of the walls, beneath the wall-walk or alure.

The irregularly shaped castle at ATHENRY (Co. Galway),
said to have been erected by de Bermingham in 1238, three
years after Richard de Burgh's invasion of Connaught, has
lost its gate-tower and a great part of its curtain walls, but
retains its keep. Assignable to *circa* 1250, this rectangular
building (Fig. 23) is still very well preserved. It is isolated
from the walls but lies close to the northern curtain. The
lowest of its three storeys is vaulted on square pillars and the
main apartment or hall above is entered by a doorway of
unusual elaboration (Fig. 24). Its moulded arch, which is
pointed in form, is borne by engaged-columns with delicately
carved capitals. The window embrasures of this room

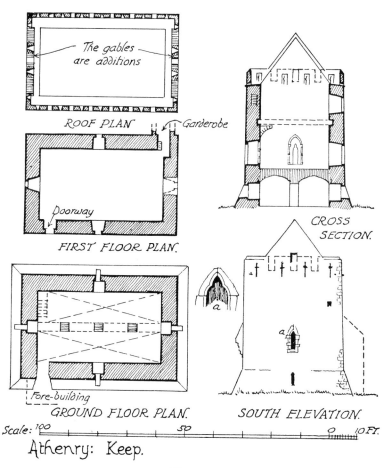

The gables
are additions

ROOF PLAN

Garderobe

FIRST FLOOR PLAN.

Doorway

CROSS
SECTION.

GROUND FLOOR PLAN.

Fore-building

SOUTH ELEVATION.

Scale: 100   50   0   10 FT.

Athenry: Keep.

Fig. 23.

The original roof proves to have been at the second floor level. A second outlet for water should appear in the south elevation balancing that shown, which was covered by ivy when the drawing was made. The vaulting is an insertion.

Athenry

Fig. 24.

also have similar columns, with banded shafts, moulded bases and carved capitals (Fig. 25), while the windows themselves have elegant trefoil-pointed heads. As the once timber-floored topmost storey is not accessible, the details of the battlements cannot be closely seen but long, narrow, cross-form loops are evident enough. So also are the high-pitched gables which, with the bold base-batter and subtle upward tapering of the walls, give the keep its distinctive character and picturesque appearance. The gables however are an addition to the original building.

ATHENRY CASTLE, Co GALWAY
WINDOW DETAILS

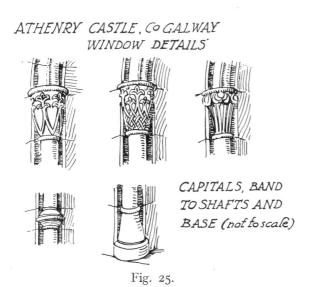

CAPITALS, BAND TO SHAFTS AND BASE (not to scale)

Fig. 25.

The keep at GREENCASTLE (Co. Down), which also appears to have stood within the curtain walls, is a long rectangle in plan, measuring 70 feet by 40 feet. Like that at Athenry it had a roof of rather steep pitch, but the gables were almost completely masked by the high parapets and not exposed as in the Galway example. The construction of this part of the castle is unusual, perhaps unique. Between the slightly projecting square turrets which rise from the ground at each corner of the building, is a high wall containing a mural passage ; the inner part of this wall rises as a gable while the outer part forms a crenellated parapet to the alure. The alures (wall-walks) of the longer walls are at the level of the mural passages mentioned and had high parapets. It is unfortunate that the windows of this keep have been greatly widened and altered but the general effect of the building is still striking and military—a massive block, culminating at each of its corners in a high, square, crenellated turret.

Plate 11

SHANID : THE KEEP

IV

CASTLES WITH
ROUND OR POLYGONAL KEEPS.

The round keep, " donjon," or " juliet " is rather less common in Ireland than in England or France. The fashion did not persist for a long period and the occurrence of the round keep, in this country, may generally be regarded as proof of an early date, round about the first decade of the thirteenth century.

The round keep at DUNDRUM (Co. Down), stands within and a little distance away from the curtains, which enclose an irregular space, bounded by a rock-cut fosse. It is four storeys high and about 45 feet in external diameter above the boldly battered base, while its present height is about equal to its width. This height may have been greater ; the ground has certainly risen and there is a possibility that the keep had its own encircling fosse. In the wall of the topmost storey are continuous mural chambers or passages.

The curtain walls, as in many, indeed most, of the earlier castles, have no projecting towers ; that form of necessary flanking defence had not yet come into general use at the time of its building. It would seem, indeed, that the early stone walls at Dundrum and other places, simply followed the lines, and took the place of the original timber palisades.

At SHANID (Co. Limerick), (Fig. 2), there are the remains of another keep, not circular but polygonal, also standing within, but close to, the curtains which surround the top of a large mote about 63 feet in diameter. A fosse and outer bank of earth surround the mote. Only part of the keep, about one half, remains to its full height of about 35 feet, including the parapets. It is circular internally, 22 feet in diameter, and has walls 11 feet in thickness. The curtains are but 5 feet thick and 16 feet high but still retain some of their battlements and loop-holes. On lower ground there is a D-shaped bailey with its own rampart and fosse. The castle is an interesting instance of stone building on a pre-existing mote, perhaps formed out of a natural hillock, which, rather than the piled-up earth, may support the later erection of stone. Shanid is not mentioned before 1230, but the structure may be considerably earlier in date. It is apparently a juliet within a shell-keep, after the manner of Launceston Castle, Cornwall.

The bridge-head castle of ATHLONE boasts another polygonal and isolated keep, or rather the remains of one, for both castle and keep have undergone many changes since about 1210, when John de Grey, the Justiciar, built it and a bridge over the Shannon at Athlone. It is probable that Geoffrey de Costentin, who was granted a cantred in Roscommon opposite Athlone in 1200, raised a mote there and likely that he re-modelled and scarped an esker or gravel ridge, one of the chain on which Athlone itself, and the fortifications of the Napoleonic period, now stand, though on opposite banks of the river. De Grey seems to have converted this into a stone walled fortress, revetting the mound with strong walls and building a tower. This tower may have been that built on the earthen mote itself, a too fresh and therefore unstable support, since the tower fell––as the Annals of Clonmacnoise record—in 1211, killing Richard Tuite and eight Englishmen with him.

There is a good deal recorded about Athlone Castle. It was repaired in 1251, and between 1273 and 1279. Probably the three-quarter-round flanking towers of the curtain were built about these times. Both these, and the keep, have been so altered that it is not possible to say how much is old and how much is comparatively modern. So lately as 1683, however, there was still a quantity of ancient work to be seen, and the whole castle, standing at the head of the famous old bridge—which lay to the southwards of the present erection—was a most picturesque and formidable pile, as befitted the gateway into Connaught.

At CASTLEKNOCK (Co. Dublin) only a tree clad mound and some shattered walls mark the site of the great castle of the Tyrells. Fortunately there is a pictorial record of how it appeared at the end of the seventeenth century. Francis Place's sketch, made in 1689 (Fig. 26), shows a large polygonal keep crowning what was seemingly a mote and forming a part of the outer defences. The lower walls in the view may represent a regular bailey walled in in later times.

Castleknock in 1698. (from drawing by Francis Place.)

Fig. 26.

NENAGH Castle, in County Tipperary, has the finest cylindrical keep in Ireland (Fig. 27). Like the many-sided keep at Castleknock, it formed part of the perimeter of the fortress, being incorporated in the curtains surrounding a rather small, five-sided courtyard (Fig. 28). These walls have almost disappeared, but the fragments remaining, together with the notes made by the Ordnance surveyors a hundred years ago, make a reasonably accurate restoration possible. There were four flanking towers, one on each side of the entrance gateway to the south, the others at the east and west angles of the pentagon ; the great keep, " Nenagh Round," occupied the northern angle (Fig. 29). Built of limestone rubble, irregularly coursed, and measuring about 55 feet in external diameter at the base, it rises now to a height of about a hundred feet. The topmost quarter,

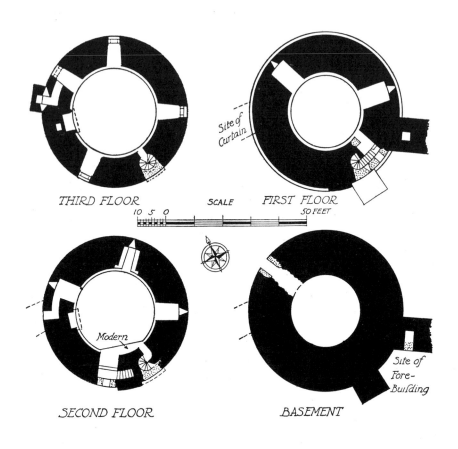

THIRD FLOOR

SCALE

FIRST FLOOR

10 5 0   50 FEET

Site of
Curtain

SECOND FLOOR

Modern

BASEMENT

Site of
Fore-
Building

Fig. 27.

Nenagh Castle. Circular Keep.

Plan of the four storeys.

however, is modern (*circa* 1860), the original height to the wall-walk being about 75 feet. Above this there rose, of course, the crenellated parapets. There were four storeys, including a basement which was approachable, originally, only from the entrance storey above. At the base the walls are 16 feet thick, and at the top, just 11 feet ; the diminishing thickness is accounted for by the inward " batter " of the walls and the offset or setting back, at each floor level, which bore the timber work of the floors. The entrance doorway—

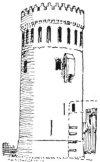

Nenagh Keep.

Fig. 29.

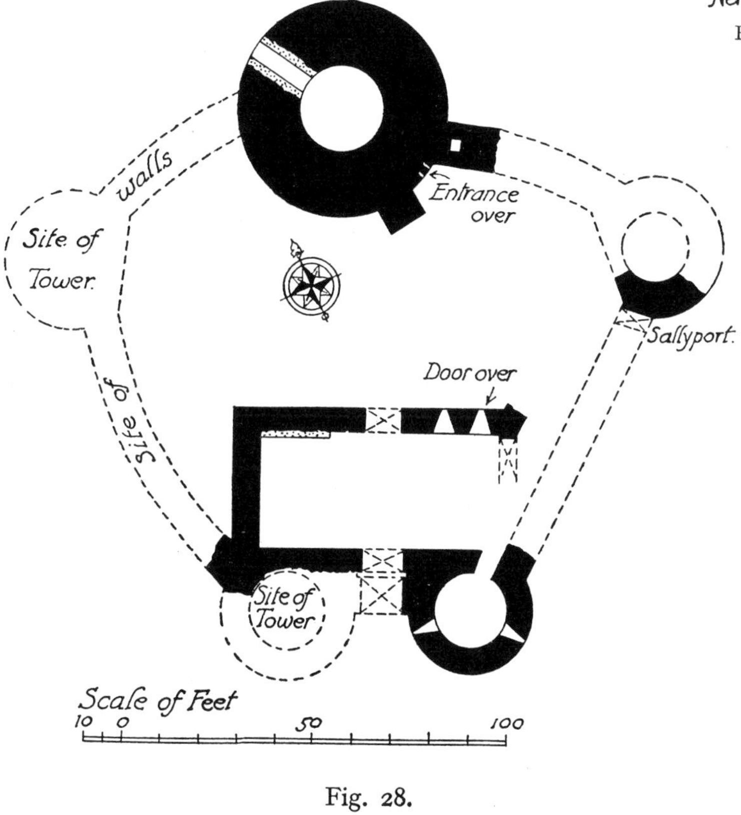

Fig. 28.

Nenagh Castle, Plan.

obliterated by modern re-buildings—was at the first floor
level and from it there still rises a winding stairs, in the
thickness of the wall, leading to all the floors and the roof.
This stairs has been altered and rather straitened by a re-
building of the outer face of the wall ; there was originally a
slightly projecting turret to accommodate it.

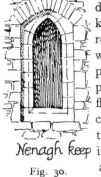

The long, narrow archery loops of the first and second
storeys, passing down well below the floors to permit of a
descending fire on assailants, are noteworthy features of the
keep. They have wide internal embrasures, almost small
rooms, for the cross-bowmen. The upper, the third floor,
windows (Fig. 30) are relatively large and have bluntly
pointed arches of wrought sandstone, set within segmental-
pointed embrasures in the rougher limestone. On the second
floor there is a wide and round-headed embrasure with a
chevron-ornamented arch in the style of *circa* 1200. Though
there are some other later features, fireplaces and the like,
Nenagh Keep it is to this date that the erection of the great keep must be
assigned, and to the energy of Theobald Walter, first of the
Butlers of Ormond.

Fig. 30.

" There are scanty remains of a small round keep at the
north end of Mannin Lough, Co. Mayo. It was about 20 feet
in internal diameter, with walls 6 feet thick and half-round
turrets to the north-west and south, besides what appears to
have been a square fore-building on the east face. Traces of
a paved fosse, within a curtain, remain on the south-east.
Two courtyards fill the rest of the small peninsula which has
a fosse, now dry, across the isthmus." —*Jr. Galway Archæological Society, vii, 117-120.*

V

THE TOWERED OR TURRETED KEEPS.

These keeps are not to be confused with the larger square or more or less rectangular castles which have circular towers at the angles of the area enclosed by the curtain walls. It is the form of the keep itself which characterizes the type : a strong rectangular tower, two or three storeys in height, provided with a massive turret rising from the ground at each of its four corners.

The keeps of this form seem to be peculiar to Ireland in the first half of the thirteenth century ; they seem to have had no forerunners in England or France and the few extant English examples belong to the following century. Those that remain in Ireland are greatly ruined but the plan and much of the detail is recoverable from the fragments.

The earliest in date is CARLOW. At this important strategic point on the River Barrow, and the borders of his fief, Hugh de Lacy erected a fortress, probably of the mote-and-bailey type. Carlow appears first in the Patent Rolls at 1231, but the keep (Fig. 31), half of which remains, is certainly earlier than this date. The name of its builder is not recorded, but it seems most likely that William Marshall the elder, raised the keep at some time between 1207 and 1213, the period which he spent continuously in Ireland. In plan (Fig. 32) it was a perfect rectangle with walls 9 feet in thickness. Attached to each corner was a nearly circular tower, about 15 feet in diameter ; these four towers gave

Carlow Castle from a print of circa 1791

Fig. 31.

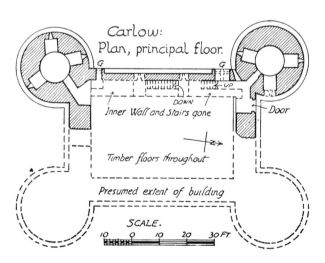

Carlow:
Plan, principal floor.

DOWN

UP

Inner Wall and Stairs gone

Door

Timber floors throughout

Presumed extent of building

SCALE.

10   0   10   20   30 FT.

Fig. 32.

flanking defence to every face of the building. The upper
floors and roof of its three storeys were of timber, stone
vaultings being absent, even in the corner towers where they
could easily have been constructed. As in most keeps the
entrance doorway, spanned by a pointed arch in this instance,
was at the level of the first floor. Being close to the north-
west tower, it was well protected and does not seem to have
had any fore-building. Access to the upper floors and roof,
and downwards to the lowest storey, was by way of stone
stairways in the thickness of the long western wall. Traces
of these stairways are visible despite the destruction of the
inner two-thirds of this wall which occurred in the early part
of last century. At this time also, one half of the keep fell
and has since been removed. Original openings are few and
very simple, mere narrow loops. The keep is, of course, but
one part of the fortress which for centuries commanded the
crossing of the Barrow. About the year 1300 there were at
Carlow, historical references tell us, a hall, a kitchen and a
prison, besides palisades of some sort. All these buildings
and the curtain walls which enclosed them, have quite
disappeared from a site given up to houses and factories.

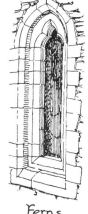

Ferns

Fig. 33.

The finest of the towered keeps is at FERNS (Co.
Wexford). That amongst the numerous references to Ferns
there are none to tell us who built it or when it was raised is
very surprising. There was certainly a manor and castle
there in 1232 when Ferns was part of the dower of Johanna,
the widow of William Earl Marshall the younger, but the
windows of the keep (Figs. 33 and 34) and the architecture of
the remarkable chapel in it are not of so early a period, they
belong rather to the middle of the century, when the castle
was held by William de Valence, husband of the Marshall
heiress.

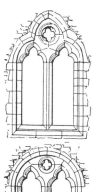

Ferns

Fig. 34.

As the three remaining towers show, Ferns keep is like
that at Carlow. It is more nearly square, however, and much
larger in dimensions, measuring internally nearly 80 feet by
60 feet and having towers of twice the diameter of those at
Carlow. The interior space must have been divided up by

partition walls, and into three storeys of large apartments, as the numerous windows show. These, which are in the upper parts of the walls, have graceful trefoil pointed heads, and are either single or grouped in pairs beneath pointed, round, or trefoil-pointed enclosing arches. No trace of the entrance doorway remains ; it must have been in one of the destroyed walls.

The most remarkable feature of the building is the chapel, on the first floor of the south-eastern tower. It is circular and is covered by a vault borne by moulded ribs, springing from corbels which are in the form of capitals with short shafts. Three single windows give light to this beautiful example of thirteenth century architecture ; the most perfect chapel to be found in any Irish castle.

At LEA, in Leix, near Portarlington, is the third of the towered keeps. Lea is often mentioned in the State Papers and seems to have had a stirring history. That it was a stronghold of the Fitzgeralds, a frontier post and a small town in the fourteenth century is clear. What is not certain is the date of its fine keep. This stands almost centrally in a roughly oval ward, commanding a much larger, and apparently later, outer walled courtyard, complete with gate-house. This outer ward extends to the bank of the river Barrow nearby.

The keep is slightly larger than that at Carlow and, like it, is oblong in plan and has its door in the same position, and a mural stairway similarly arranged. The corner towers, only one of which is still fairly complete, are bigger, being some 30 feet in external diameter. With one exception all the openings are single loops. The exception is a relatively large window consisting of a pair of trefoil-pointed lights like those of Ferns but lacking the outer casement and enclosing arch. On the evidence of this window a date of about 1250 may be assumed for the castle ; at the time when Maurice Fitzgerald, second Baron of Offaly, occupied Lea.

At a later period, probably about 1297, when the State Papers record some expenditure at " Leghe," the double-towered gate-building of the outer ward seems to have been erected. This form of structure is a feature of the late thirteenth century castles to be dealt with in greater detail hereafter. It is sufficient to say here that the Lea gateway and the works around it were much altered in later times. There is a gateway, also much ruined, between the outer and inner wards and some sections of the loop-holed and once parapeted wall of the latter.

Part of a keep of the same type remains at TERRYGLASS (Co. Tipperary), near Lough Derg, on the furthest limits of the Butler lands of Ormond and perhaps built by that great family. Only the lower storey still stands and the building may never have been more than a storey higher. The staircase is not mural, as in the other castles, but fills one of the corner towers.

At WEXFORD there was, it seems, a castle of the same type, and the picturesque building at ENNISCORTHY is most probably a re-building of *circa* 1586 on the lines of a similar towered keep.

C

VI.

CITY AND OTHER KEEPLESS CASTLES.

Though the keepless castle is characteristic of the second half of the thirteenth century, the three city castles of Dublin, Kilkenny and Limerick, built earlier in the century, seem to have lacked this feature from the first.

DUBLIN Castle, historically the most important, is the most altered of the three ; very little that is ancient remains within its Georgian facades to-day. The Wardrobe, now the Record Tower, about a hundred feet of the massive south curtain, now almost completely obscured by later buildings, the base of the Bermingham Tower, and a fragment of the gate to the city—absorbed in an eighteenth century building—are the sole remnants of this famous building.

There is a plan extant, made at the end of the seventeenth century, which shows the castle in almost its original form. Though nearly rectangular it was actually five-sided in plan. Towards the city on the west and north, the curtain walls ran originally in straight lines between the corner towers and this was also the case on the eastern side. On the south side, however, towards the fosse filled by the waters of the little river Poddle, the curtain was in two lengths meeting in an obtuse angle at a small central tower or towers. The great towers standing at the northern angles of the fortress were, like the Wardrobe Tower, cylindrical and very massive and high. That at the north-east corner was called the Storehouse Tower and appears to have been the earliest and most important, serving as a keep perhaps. It and the corresponding structure at the north-west corner, the Corke Tower, a re-building on a square plan of the original circular tower which stood on the same site, were demolished in the eighteenth century. At the same time the twin-towered gate-building, nearly midway in the north curtain, was taken down except for its western tower or turret. This, it is believed, forms the central portion of the eighteenth century building which now shelters the Office of Arms ; its thick walls surround the staircase and support the elegant tower and cupola which is the best feature of the castle of to-day.

The great south-eastern tower which houses part of the Public Records was called at different times the Wardrobe or the Gunner's Tower. It is a massive structure of limestone rubble masonry. Its walls are immensely thick and it measures about 56 feet in diameter. The machicolated parapets which crown it are not ancient, having been built so recently as 1819.

In 1775 the Fourteenth Century Bermingham Tower, at the other corner of the south curtain, was taken down and rebuilt in its present form, but it retains its battered base now hidden by more modern buildings. Eastwards from it, but also hidden, is a long length of the base of the south curtain, above which at a higher level, is the outer wall of St Patrick's Hall, an original but altered fragment. The small octagonal building, which is a feature of the present south front of the castle, probably stands on the site of a small tower or turret marking the change in the line of the south curtain at this point. The seventeenth century plan[1] : and an inventory of the towers and the loops and windows in them, which is dated 1585[2] : show that the west curtain ran from the Corke Tower to a small rectangular tower, apparently original, just west of the Bermingham Tower and joining the city wall.

---

[1] Phillips : MSS. Report on Fortifications in Ireland (1685), in Nat. Liby of Ireland

[2] Quoted by Gilbert in Calendar, vol. ii, pp. 558, ff.

Authorities differ regarding the date of the erection of Dublin Castle. The Royal Writ for the building is dated 1205 and Henry de Loundres, Archbishop of Dublin, is said to have completed the work about 1220.[1] Another authority states that only the main walls had been built by 1228 and the towers at some subsequent time.[2]

Such great buildings were not often erected at great speed in any case, but it may fairly be assumed that this fortress was completed within the first forty years of the thirteenth century.

The second of the city castles is that of LIMERICK. Stanihurst, the Elizabethan historian, states—without quoting any earlier authority —that Prince John founded an " egregium castellum " and built a bridge at Limerick. It is doubtful if any part of the existing structure is so early as 1185, when John visited Ireland as a prince, but the Irish annals speak of a " bawn " at Limerick in 1200 and of a " castle " two years later. That the castle was first built in the early years of the thirteenth century is made certain by these references and a later one, of 1216, that the building was in need of repairs.

The castle (Plan, Fig. 35), stands within the city and forming part of its extensive walled defences, commanding the approach from Thomond. Close by it to the north stood Thomond Gate at the city end of the bridge of the same name spanning Ireland's largest river. The castle is five-sided but nearly square in plan. Its western and longest side is on the river and is almost straight, joining two round towers. The more northerly tower is the stronger and was—originally— the highest and most important of the four which formed the angles of the fortress. One of them, that to the south-east, was removed, its place being taken by a large bastion built in 1611 to overawe the city. All the corner towers have been lowered to accommodate heavy artillery. Near the centre of the north side, facing Castle Street, and adjoining the short length of the curtain which starts from the north-east tower,

[1] Camden's *Britannia*.
[2] Ware's *Annals* (1705), p. 45.

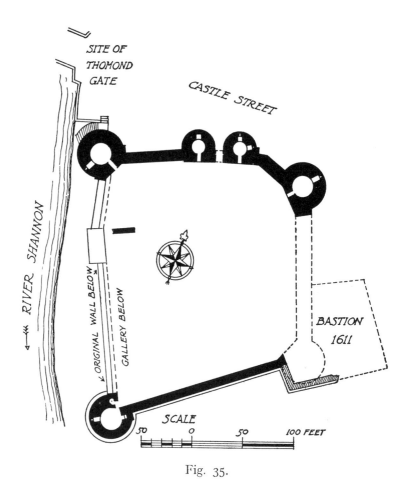

SITE OF
THOMOND
GATE

CASTLE STREET

RIVER SHANNON

ORIGINAL WALL BELOW

GALLERY BELOW

BASTION
1611

SCALE

50   0   50   100 FEET

Fig. 35.

Limerick Castle, plan.

is a twin-towered gate-building, its parts hardly less massive
than the main towers. It now presents two D-shaped towers
towards the street ; originally it projected inwards towards
the courtyard in rectangular fashion. Between the towers
is the gateway, with a pointed arch, and now approached by
a flight of steps in place of the one-time drawbridge. Within
it was a portcullis and, very probably, other doors.

The building has suffered many changes, such as the
destruction of the east curtain and south-east tower, the
insertion of heavy vaultings in the towers and the lowering
of them to support heavy guns. Finally, the building of
barracks within the castle in the eighteenth century greatly
changed the structure but the larger part of it remains ;
a splendid relic of the past. (See Plate IV.)

KILKENNY Castle was erected in the thirteenth century
on the site of Strongbow's mote fortress. In 1307, we are
told, there was " a castle in which are a hall, four towers, a
chapel, a mote and divers other houses." A nobleman's
residence from the beginning, the chief seat of the Butlers, it
has undergone many alterations, notably in 1660 and again in
the early part of the nineteenth century. The mote has
gone and with it one of the four towers which stood in 1307.
The three very massive round towers which remain—pierced
though their walls are by numerous and large modern windows—are undoubtedly ancient. So also is the main north
wall but the rest is modern though following the outline of the
old works : a four-sided, wedge-shaped castle, wider towards
the south than on the north side, with a large tower at each
angle.

There may be grouped with the city castles another of
lesser importance, the town castle of ROSCREA (Co.
Tipperary). Like several others it is attributed to King John
but is hardly earlier, in its present form, than the middle of
the thirteenth century, It has a gate tower assignable to
circa 1280. In plan the castle is a very irregular polygon,
flanked by the gate tower mentioned, which is rectangular,
and two others nearly D-shaped. Part of the south curtain

Roscrea Castle. Gate tower

Fig. 36.

wall has disappeared. There is a record of the building of a
mote at Roscrea in 1245 but no trace of this work now remains.
The most striking feature is the gate tower (Fig. 36), occupying part of the north side of the castle and owing its picturesque
quality to the gables and chimneys added in the seventeenth
century but since modified. At the lower levels the original
work is still to be seen : the pointed arches of the built-up
gateway—with the openings for the beams of the vanished
drawbridge—and a fine, vaulted apartment on the first floor in
which are the remains of a very large hooded fireplace.

VII

CASTLES ON ROCKS.

Of the keepless castles several which occupy rocky sites may be grouped together. The earliest in date seems to be that at CARLINGFORD (Co. Louth), which stands on the verge of a small cliff overlooking the harbour, between the hills and the seashore of Carlingford Lough in a strong and commanding position.

King John, who came to Carlingford in 1210 and is credited with the building of a castle at almost every place that he visited, is said to have ordered its erection. It is more than probable that there was a castle here before 1210 and that the western half of the extant works antedates John's visit. The other, the eastern part, can be dated with some certainty to the year 1261, when payments were made for the quarrying and transport of stone to both Carlingford and Greencastle on the other side of the Lough.

The plan (Fig. 37) of the castle may be described as irregularly D-shaped, with the curved part of the letter facing towards the hills to the west. A massive high wall running from north to south divides the building into two nearly equal parts. The western portion is the courtyard, enclosed by strong walls, following a very irregular line and pierced by small loops set in wide embrasures. These are disposed in two storeys, the upper row being, doubtless, accessible from a wooden gallery. In the central part of the west wall there stood an oblong gate-building of early type, pierced by a

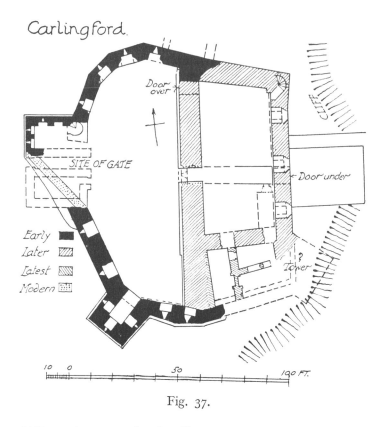

Fig. 37.

narrow gate passage, barely wide enough for a single horseman. Further to the south there is a small tower, square below but having canted angles to its upper storey, projecting from the wall. To the north there seems to have been another flanking tower. The lay-out of the western wall suggests that the early fortress may have been, broadly speaking, oval in plan. However this may have been, there can be no doubt that the eastern half of the castle, which is almost rectangular in plan, is later than the other part. It was, moreover, a roofed building of two storeys in height raised over a basement or cellars now largely filled up. The entrance doorway is on the first floor at the north corner of the courtyard (the existing ground floor entrance was originally a loop commanding the gate of the castle directly opposite) and led to what was probably the great hall of the castle. On the ground floor level were other apartments while others, smaller, filled several storeys in the south end of the building. A doorway in the basement led to a small platform on the cliff edge.

There can be little doubt that this part of the castle dates from 1261.

Commanding a pass in the hills of south Armagh, some miles north-west from Dundalk, is CASTLEROCHE, one of the most striking relics of the century. The first reference to it is an entry in the Close Rolls dated 1236. According to this, the Lady Rohesia de Verdon had fortified a castle in her own lands against the Irish, " which none of her predecessors was able to do." It is probable, however, that her son, John de Verdon, who died in 1274, was the builder of the greater part of the castle we see to-day, rising from its rocky site (Fig. 38) which is almost cliff-like on three of its sides. It had a large walled bailey, on the stony plateau to the south, separated from the castle proper by a rock-cut fosse.

Castleroche from S.

Fig. 38.

In shape the castle is peculiar, almost triangular in its plan. High curtains, which retain many of their merlons, enclose the whole, except where the gate-building and the great hall form parts of the perimeter. The former is of the double-towered type but its inner section is quite ruined. Adjoining it is the large roofless building in the upper storey of which was the hall, lighted by three large windows provided with seats.

Even more dramatically sited than Castleroche, but far less complete, is DUNAMASE (Leix), crowning a massive rock some miles east of Maryborough and commanding a gap in the hills and a vast extent of country. The castle is the Norman successor to an Irish fortress held by Leinster clans and kings from early times. Strongbow, by his marriage with Dermott MacMurrough's daughter, obtained Dunamase and it descended as did other fiefs of the intruder, to William Earl Marshall, husband of a Strongbow heiress. It is recorded that William de Braose or Bruce rebuilt and enlarged Dunamase about the year 1250, while that other powerful noble, Roger de Mortimer, is also credited with building there. Though reduced to a shattered ruin by the Cromwellian generals, Hewson and Reynolds, in 1650, and by time and weather since then, the outlines of the fortress are clear. On the east, the lowest and most accessible side, is a D-shaped bailey and west of this a walled outer courtyard, triangular in shape. This, entered by way of a round-faced gate tower (Fig 39) which has traces of a drawbridge, slopes upward to the inner ward, a terraced heart-shaped area crowning the rock. The main gate-building in the centre of the inner curtain is greatly mutilated. It has lost its whole outer face but seems to have been oblong in shape, with guard rooms on each side of the entrance passage. Irregular towerless curtains enclose the ward and a much broken rectangular keep—which bears evidences of alterations of so late a period as the sixteenth century, but is in part of thirteenth century date—occupies the highest part of the rock. Some traces of walling suggest that this part was divided by a cross wall from the rest of the

Dunamase Gateway

Fig. 39.

Plate III

"KING JOHN'S" CASTLE
CARLINGFORD

CARRIGOGUNNELL

ward and formed an inner courtyard associated with the keep itself.

CASTLECONNELL (Co. Limerick) also stands upon a rock but its shattered state and the luxuriant growth upon its walls prevents a critical examination. It appears to have been rectangular.

Of all the rock sited castles none can be more picturesque than DUNLUCE (Co. Antrim) standing on its precipitous, isolated and seagirt rock, the site of an early fort as the name denotes ; the existence there of a rock-cut souterrain yielding pottery of *circa* 400 B.C. is corroborative. Dunluce may have been built by Richard de Burgh, Earl of Ulster—or by one of his men—about 1300, but it is not impossible that the first foundation may be somewhat earlier. The earliest works remaining are two cylindrical towers—NE. and SE.—and most of the south curtain of what seems to have been, originally, a four-sided and more or less rectangular fortress with strong towers at the angles. Only a very small part of the foundation of the east curtain survives, the rest having fallen, along with the cliff face which supported it, while within the south curtain are the remains of an arcaded gallery—a unique feature. At the S.W. angle is a large rectangular gatehouse of *circa* 1600, still crowned at the outer angles by round turrets of Scottish type (*infra* Fig. 96, p. 138). Of about the same period are the very extensive remains of domestic buildings, a veritable English manor-house, occupying the greater part of the original courtyard and extending northwards beyond it. They comprise a great hall (which had three bay-windows), a parlour, kitchen, and buttery, the last named being of somewhat earlier date than the rest. Northwards again lies a lower court, oblong and bordered by lesser buildings while on the mainland, south of the deep isolating gap, lie very extensive but now formless buildings of Jacobean date.

Little is known of Dunluce's history from its foundation until early in the XVIth century, when the McQuillans held it, to be succeeded by Colla MacDonnell and, subsequently, by the redoubtable Sorley Boy MacDonnell, his brother. Shane O'Neill took the castle but Sorley returned. Elizabeth's Lord Deputy, Sir John Perrott took it in 1584 and in the Rebellion of 1641 it was unsuccessfully besieged. Since that time it has ceased to be a residence of the Earls of Antrim.

VIII

THE KEEPLESS CASTLES
OF THE LATER 13TH CENTURY.

Though castles without keeps were built, as has been shown, in the first half of the century, the keep was a normal and usual feature so late as 1250. In the castles built after that date, however, it is no longer found. On the other hand, the towers projecting from the curtain walls grow in size and number, affording an increasing degree of flanking defence to the walls that stretch between them.

Perhaps the most notable feature of the later castles is the gate-building, usually a massive structure ; a rectangle from which project outwards a pair of half-round towers. Between these is the gateway of the castle, opening into a passage passing through the whole width of the building. The towers not only guard the main entrance but afford a flanking defence to the curtains on each side of the gate-house.

Gate-buildings of this kind were added to the early castles of Dundrum, Lea and Castleroche and are found also in the city castles of Dublin and Limerick. At Nenagh, where two round towers seem to have flanked the original gate from the beginning, a rectangular building was erected at the back of them later, within the gateway.

It is at ROSCOMMON (Plan Fig. 40), however, that the finest twin-towered gate-building is to be found, though in a far from complete condition. It is the largest unit in the

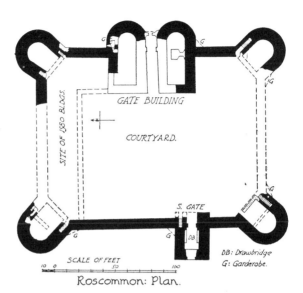

Fig. 40.

castle, whose four curtains enclose a spacious, nearly rectangular, courtyard measuring 162 feet by 130 feet. At each
corner of the castle is a bold and high tower, D-shaped in
plan. The gate-building is placed astride the east curtain in
its centre, the two rounded towers projecting almost as far
outwards as does its much ruined oblong inner part into the
courtyard. Between the towers was the gateway, at the outer
end of a passage barely ten feet in width. Like the other
towers of the castle the gate structure was originally three
storeys in height, but like two of them and other parts of the
castle, it underwent many alterations about 1580. At this
time the number of floors was increased and the early, narrow
windows and loops much enlarged. The way in which this
was done in the towers is of considerable interest : the old
wide inner embrasures of the windows were made into continuous tall gaps by the removal of the outer walls and the
stonework at each floor, and in these gaps the present
mullioned and transomed windows have been built. The

effect of these alterations was to make the building more modern and lightsome but less defensible. At the same period extensive buildings, now gone, were erected within the castle at its north end.

Other parts of the structure were not affected by the new works of the sixteenth century. The southern flanking towers (Fig. 41), the western gate and curtains, though damaged and broken, remain essentially unchanged. Each of the corner towers is shaped like an elongated D, with its straight bar facing the courtyard, and each has a mural stairway. The west curtain, 9 feet in thickness, has no openings, but has lost its crenellated parapet, while the oblong building of the west gate still has its vaulted passage and traces of a counter-balance drawbridge.

Corner Tower and squinch: Roscommon

Fig. 41.

The confused records show that Roscommon was a royal castle, built or restored by Robert de Ufford, the Justiciary, about the year 1280, in the place of earlier works begun by him in 1269. Several of these appear to have been destroyed by the O'Connors. For nearly thirty years it was held by a government garrison, but, between that time and the middle of the sixteenth century, it often changed hands. Indeed, the O'Connors seem to have held it for the greater part of the time. In 1569 the Lord Deputy, Sydney, secured Roscommon and it was granted, nine years later, to Sir Nicholas Malbie. He it was, it seems, who carried out the alterations which have given Roscommon something of the aspect of a many-windowed French chateau. In 1652 its career as a place of strength was closed by the Cromwellian general, Reynolds, who effectively dismantled the once great fortress.

Some ten miles from Roscommon is BALLINTUBBER, another castle on the same general lines but larger and different in its details ; its corner towers, for instance, are polygonal instead of D-shaped. Built about 1300 by the O'Connors and held by them for centuries, Ballintubber seems to be an Irish copy of Roscommon.

The most symmetrical castle of the keepless type is that at BALLYMOTE (Co. Sligo) (Fig. 42). It was built about the

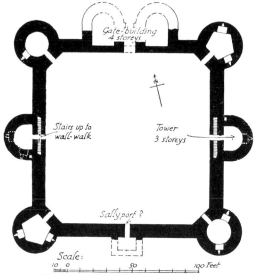

Ballymote: Sketch Plan (not surveyed).

Fig. 42.

year 1300 by Richard de Burgh at some distance from an earlier mote castle erected, probably, by an earlier **Burke**. Almost square in plan, with a massive three-quarter-round tower at each angle, it had a double-towered gate-building of great size. This formidable gate stood in the centre of the north curtain but has lost all but the foundations of its towers. There are smaller towers placed mid-way in the other curtains ; those to the east and west being D-shaped, while that to the south was square in plan, covering a postern gate. The curtains are about ten feet in thickness and have mural stairways leading to the wall tops above which level the various towers rose to a greater height. In its heyday Ballymote must have been a very striking building ; though still massive and strong it has lost the towers of its great gatehouse and is heavily mantled in ivy.

Another castle of very symmetrical plan is QUIN (Co. Clare), built by de Clare in 1278-80 and destroyed by Cuvea

Macnamara in 1288. About a century and a half later its ruins were put to a new use by the Franciscan Order whose friars erected upon and within the old walls, a friary of remarkable interest and beauty. Looking down to-day from the top of the slender belfry of the friary church the outline of a great part of the castle can be seen. It was square in plan with massive round towers at each of its angles and had curtain walls 11 feet thick. One of these became, with alterations, the south wall of the church, the others bear the foundations of the friary walls. The lower parts of three of the towers still remain, but one, that to the north-west, has quite disappeared. So also have all traces of the gateway and the other buildings which must have occupied some part of the square within the walls.

CASTLEGRACE (Tipperary), though not dissimilar in plan to Quin, is smaller and less strong. It was oblong in shape and had the usual corner towers, of which one was square. Within its west curtain were buildings in which there is one window of the type found at Ferns, suggesting a date not much later than 1250. Nothing is recorded of its history but that the feudal barony in which it stood once belonged to the Wigornias or Worcester family, and later to the de Berminghams who may have raised the castle.

Another castle consisting of a large rectangular courtyard with corner towers, but a larger building than either Quin or Castlegrace, stands at LISCARROLL in northern Cork. Its towers must have been rather inadequate flanking defences to the very long east and west curtains but the shorter walls on the south and north were well defended by intermediate towers : a square one to the north and a strong, oblong gate tower in the centre of the south wall. This tower, which has been much altered in its upper parts, still retains the entrance passage and traces of the heavy doors and portcullises which barred the ingress of an intruder. On each side of the tower, within the courtyard, there were once large buildings but there are no traces of any others in the very spacious interior. History is silent as to the date of the foundation of this

fortress ; it may have been built by the de Barrys, who held
this part of Cork, at some time in the later thirteenth century.

Much smaller and most irregular in its plan is the castle
of the MacJordans (descendants of Jordan de Exeter) at
BALLYLAHAN in Mayo.   It had a double-towered gate-
building but apparently possessed no flanking towers, a lack
suggesting an earlier date for the main structure than for the
gate-building, which can hardly be earlier than about 1260.

BALLYLOUGHAN (Co. Carlow) (Fig. 43), also has a
gate-building of this form, the towers of which, however, are
nearly circular and project to the sides as well as the front.
Enough of the extensive main structure remains to show
that, apart from the gate structure, it was not very strongly
defended.   A low, square tower of small height with a pair of
pointed windows placed rather near the ground, stood at one
angle of the enclosure, and was apparently balanced by
similar buildings at the other corners.   The buildings are
liberally provided with interesting fireplaces (Fig. 58).

Ballyloughan: gateway –
features restored

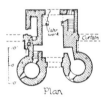

Plan

Fig. 43.

The remains of thirteenth century castles at other places
in Ireland are, in most cases, less perfect or important than
those so far described and can receive but brief mention here.

At SWORDS (Co. Dublin) is an episcopal castle, begun
about 1200.   It is manorial in its character and not very strong
in the military sense, though large in area and still completely
walled on all sides.   A picturesque building, with a chapel
adjoined, guards the gateway and a small tower projects from
the northern part of its five-sided perimeter.   Neither of these
buildings is so early as 1200—the chapel is, indeed, probably
of the fourteenth century—but there stood, on the east side,
a hall building of the later part of the thirteenth century.
Stepped battlements, typical of the fifteenth century, crown
the curtain walls.

CLONMORE Castle (Co. Carlow) is much ruined but still
retains some windows of thirteenth century type, trefoil-
pointed lights in pairs.   At ARDRAHAN (Co. Galway) and
CLONMACNOISE (Offaly) are the remains of square keeps,

both built upon earthworks and, therefore, possibly of some time about the middle of the century. Round castles remain at ARDFINNAN[1] (Co. Tipperary), CLOUGHOUTER (Co. Cavan) and AGHADOE (Co. Kerry), while KILTINANE (Co. Tipperary) is quadrangular and has three angle towers.

The examples described—the more important military relics of the thirteenth century—illustrate castle development during the period, but fragments of others remain in a more ruinous condition or incorporated in later buildings. The century was, in Ireland, pre-eminently the period of the large castles. The succeeding hundred years produced no buildings,

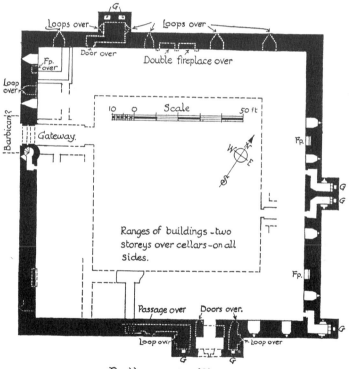

Ballymoon: Plan

Fig. 44.

[1] See note on next page.

military, domestic or ecclesiastical on the same scale. It was
not entirely barren, however, in military building for there is
one remarkable, indeed unique, castle which may be dated
with reasonable certainty to about the year 1310, Ballymoon,
in County Carlow. Nothing is known of the history of
BALLYMOON Castle (Plan Fig. 44). It has been attributed,
without authority, to the Knights Templars, who never held
land in the vicinity. Almost an exact square in plan,
surrounded by walls of granite 8 feet in thickness and about
20 feet in height, it crowns a small eminence. From three of
its faces small, oblong towers project and afford some flanking
protection, but the west curtain—which contains the gateway—has no such defence. It may have existed in the form
of a barbican to the gate. This has segmental-pointed arches,
besides grooves and a recess for the portcullis. Around the
interior on all sides there were—or were intended to be;
according to local tradition the castle was never inhabited—
ranges of buildings, as is evident from the window embrasures,
doors, fireplaces, garderobes and the like which remain in the
walls.[2] Many of these features are still quite perfect—the
segmental-pointed arches to the window embrasures, the
" Caernarvon " arches to the doorways, and the cross form
loops. These (as Fig. 11) are circularly expanded at the top,
bottom, and sides to increase the field of fire. Similar loops
remain at Ferns, which is earlier, but the form remained in
use for some centuries.

[1] Austin Cooper's drawing of Ardfinnan (1785) shows the large tower
in the back-ground and a rectangular tower at the south-east angle,
rising to a storey higher on the east face, as in Burnchurch (p. 89), while,
extending westwards, is a long wall within which rise two high gables,
apparently those of a hall.

[2] Not shown on the plan of Ballymoon are traces of some windows and,
possibly, of a mural passage in the west wall near the south-west angle,
and a loop and small window with a pointed arch not far south of the
gateway in the same wall.

IX

THE TOWER HOUSES.

As has been said already, the fourteenth century in Ireland—after its first two decades at least—was not a period of much building activity. Castles were repaired and, doubtless, altered but no major work, in its entirety, can be assigned to the years from 1320 to the end of the century. The great rock castle of Carrigogunnel in County Limerick, for instance, which from the south looks like a tremendous battleship for ever moving down the Shannon, is mentioned about 1339, but the greater part of its remains are not earlier than the fifteenth century.

From about 1440 onwards there was a great building revival, signalized especially by the addition of belfry towers and cloister arcades to the monasteries and the erection of completely new houses for the Friars—both Franciscan and Dominican—particularly in the western parts of the country. About the middle of the century the laymen seem to have begun to build for themselves and for another hundred and fifty years or more they kept the masons hard at work.

It is to this period that by far the greater number of the single towers—fortified residences, tower houses, belong. They are very numerous and are quite the most evident ancient features of the Irish countryside. Rich lands have, as might be expected, the greater numbers ; Limerick alone had not less than 400 of all dates. Clare 120, Tipperary at least 253 and Cork not less than 325. (*See Appendix.*)

Though not comparable in massiveness with the military erections of the first period, which seem to have served their primary purpose in the succeeding periods, the later castles possessed sufficient defensive power, none the less, to withstand the raids and forays of the times. They are really fortified houses, the ordinary and typical residences of the Irish and Anglo-Irish gentry. That homes so ill-lighted and still fortress-like continued to be built even to so late a time as the beginning of the seventeenth century, after the time when its English equivalent had become a many-windowed manor house or " hall "—" more glass than wall "—illustrates the contrast in the internal conditions of the two countries.

For the most part the minor castles find no place in historic record. All must have a history, be it no more than the story of their inhabitants, but of few is there much known. Indeed, it is not too much to say that those castles which survive in more or less good condition to-day do so because their histories have been uneventful, or that many which have disappeared or now lie in shapeless ruin have an unhappy record.

How or where the tower house type originated is not clear. In a sense they are small keeps, thinner walled, less fortress-like than the early examples. It has been fashionable to call them pele-towers or peels, after the borderholds, so misnamed, of Northumbria, to some of which they bear a resemblance, though not a strong one. The " peles " appear, however, to be contemporaneous, generally, with the Irish towers and can hardly have served as models for them. Moreover they derive their popular name from the piles or palisades of the strong places which preceded them in date. An origin for the Irish towers might be sought in what were called " the £10 castles." These were the fruit of a statute of the 8th year of Henry VI (1429) which states :—" It is agreed and asserted that every liege-man of our Lord the King of the said counties (viz., Dublin, Meath, Kildare, and Louth, counties of the English Pale) who chooses to build a castle or tower sufficiently embattled or fortified within the next ten years to wit twenty feet in length sixteen feet in width and forty feet in height or more, that the Commons of the said counties shall pay to the said person to build the said castle or tower ten pounds by way of subsidy." Later in the reign another act laid down minimum internal dimensions of fifteen feet by twelve feet for the £10 castles of Meath, and in 1449 a limit was put to the numbers to be built. There is a very simple tower at DONORE (Fig. 45), near Killyon in County Meath, which adheres closely in its inside measurements and height to the requirements of the statute of 1429. It has lost the wrought stonework from its door and window openings and also its battlements. It has a vault over the two lower storeys as have most of the simple towers. Each of its external corners is rounded and in one of them is a winding stair in a turret, leading to the two upper storeys and the roof. Its very simplicity suggests an early date but its claim to be the progenitor of the towers is not conclusive.

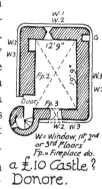

a £.10 Castle? Donore.

Fig. 45.

Less simple in plan, and much more picturesque in appearance, are the small castles of County Down, notably that at KILCLIEF (Fig. 46) ascribed with good reason to John Cely, Bishop of Down between 1412 and 1441. This tower has two towers or turrets projecting from one of its faces. They rise from the ground to some height over the embattled parapets of the main structure, as do also two other small turrets at the other corners of the building. One of the projecting turrets encloses a winding stairs, the other small

Kilclief

Fig. 46.

chambers and a garderobe with its shaft.   Spanning the space between the turrets is a bold arch beneath the main battlements; in effect this feature is a machicolation defending the entrance doorway three storeys below, close to the stairs turret.   The walls of Kilclief have a graceful batter and retain part of their crowning features—the picturesque stepped battlements.

Other small castles in Down follow the same plan.   In Louth and Meath are others not unlike the Down types, but in them a single projecting turret—containing the winding stairs—is not uncommon, while two or four turrets, rising from the ground at the angles, are often found but appear to be a mark of a relatively late date.

At ROODSTOWN (Co. Louth), (Fig. 47), there is a small tower with two turrets, which are in plan prolongations of the side walls.

The £10 castles seem to have been designed as defences for the Pale counties rather than as houses, but the towers most often found are more ambitious, of larger dimensions and more liveable.   By far the greater number of these " castles " or towers present the same external appearance

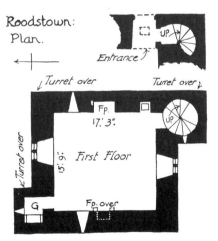

Fig. 47.

and have a standard internal arrangement with slight variations in detail between one and another. They are simple oblongs within four walls, subtly battered, rising sheerly from a bold base-batter, to parapets which are crenellated in the Irish fashion. A small turret at one corner, generally above the staircase, rises to a greater height than the rest of the building, while within the parapets are the two gables of the roof. Very often a small machicolation projects from the parapet and commands the entrance doorway below ; similar features may be found at one or more of the angles of the building.

This simple exterior clothes a quite complicated interior arrangement consisting of two main vertical divisions : one comprising the entrance, the winding stairs and a number of small chambers ; the other made up of the larger rooms. The division is not usually expressed outside in any marked way except in some of the Clare, Galway and Limerick castles where a joint is visible between the two sections and may indicate that the narrower part was built first.

The general arrangement of the inside of these towers can best be illustrated from an actual and nearly perfect example, built in the late fifteenth century but upon the standard plan which subsisted for quite two centuries : the castle at CLARA, County Kilkenny (Figs. 48-51).

On the left hand of the entrance lobby a short passage leads to a winding stairs occupying one corner of the building and rising to the topmost room, while, to the right is a small dark chamber, perhaps for the door-keeper. Facing the entrance another door leads into a room, very dimly lighted by small loops set in deep embrasures. At Clara the floor over this room is of wood but in many castles the space is vaulted over in stone. In all cases it seems to have been used as a store or cellar, it was certainly too dark and gloomy for any other purpose.

The winding stairs of stone, lighted by many slit windows, leads up to the doorway of a large room over the cellar and, on the same or a slightly higher level to another, smaller,

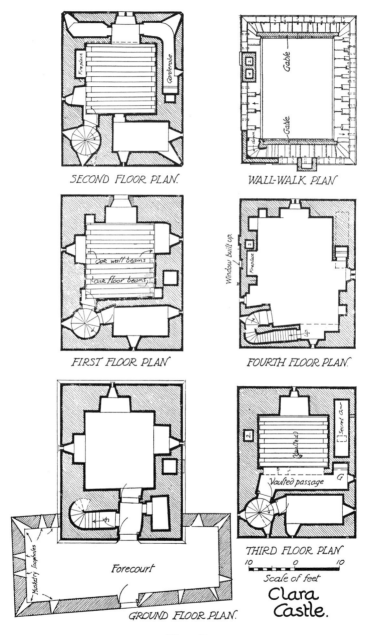

SECOND FLOOR PLAN.

WALL-WALK PLAN

FIRST FLOOR PLAN

FOURTH FLOOR PLAN.

GROUND FLOOR PLAN.

THIRD FLOOR PLAN

Scale of feet

Clara Castle.

Fig. 48.

doorway giving access to a long but narrow chamber over the entrance lobby and porter's room. In the larger room are several wall cupboards and loop windows, narrow but somewhat larger than those in the cellar below, while in the stone floor of the narrow chamber is the " murdering hole," commanding the lobby below ; through it, with arrow, spear or—later—firearm of some kind, the defender had at his mercy anyone who had managed to force an entrance.

On the next storey are two more rooms of the same size as those below, but better lighted and better suited for living in. The larger room contains a fireplace while passages in the thickness of its walls lead to a garderobe and defensive loops in the angles of the tower. The two rooms forming, as it were, a self-contained suite, were evidently those occupied by the head of the house ; the smaller one, which is not entered from the staircase, being, in all probability, a sleeping chamber. The ceiling of the large room is a vault of stone, high enough to provide a sort of attic. This is entered from a passage which leads across from the staircase to another mural garderobe, and at the same level there is another narrow chamber like that below. Hidden behind the vaulting on one side there is a secret chamber, to which access can be gained only by an opening masquerading as a garderobe seat, beside the large room occupying the whole top storey of the castle.

This latter is undoubtedly the most important room in the building—the general living and cooking place. Its windows are the largest in the castle ; there are three wall-cupboards, a large fireplace and a slop-stone delivering through the wall below a window. In the timber roof above there was a small attic or loft.

The winding stairs stops at this storey and a narrower, nearly straight, mural stair takes its place and leads to the roof-walks by way of the turret—a sort of bulkhead or companion-way of stone at the corner of the building over the main stairs. This turret breaks the continuity of the walk or alure, which is otherwise practically clear and unobstructed

on its way around the gables. The alure serves the double
purpose of gutter and defence.

The structure and its features have many points of
interest.   Like most other Irish buildings of the period it is
built of limestone—unwrought or merely hammer dressed
rubble in the walls, of chiselled stone at the quoins or corners,
and about the doors and windows. In the sixteenth century
the wrought stones were often further ornamented with
punchings of dots in varied patterns.

The arches, within and without, are made up, not of
regular voussoirs, but of a few large stones ; the windows, on
the other hand, are for the most part square-headed and show
the graceful ogee curve, either plain or wrought into cusps.
Small round-headed windows also occur. Almost all
the openings are chamfered round about on the outside. This
has a curious effect where the opening, door or window, is
in the bold batter at the base of the building : the chamfer
splays out widely downwards and gives a tapering effect to
the whole opening. The larger windows, or those at some
distance above the ground, are, in some cases, set back in a
slight recess or casement and crowned by a moulded hood.
This bends downwards at each side and finishes in tapered
fashion and either in a point or a carved vine leaf or flower in
relief. The later hood-mouldings often lack such ornament
and finish squarely. A general view of the castle from the
south-east is given in Figure 50, while Figure 51 shows two
of its elevations—with the position of the secret chamber—
and some details, including a typical upper window.

In Clara Castle the heavy oak timbers of the floors remain
in position, an unusual survival. The beams or joists are
twelve or fourteen inches wide and rest on other timbers of the
same size, called wall-plates, which lie close to the wall and
are borne by stone corbels. This (Fig. 49) is the usual
arrangement. When looking at a floorless castle to-day, the
observer must picture in his mind the missing floor levels at
from twenty inches to two feet over the corbels which still
jut out from the walls. See Figure 62 also.

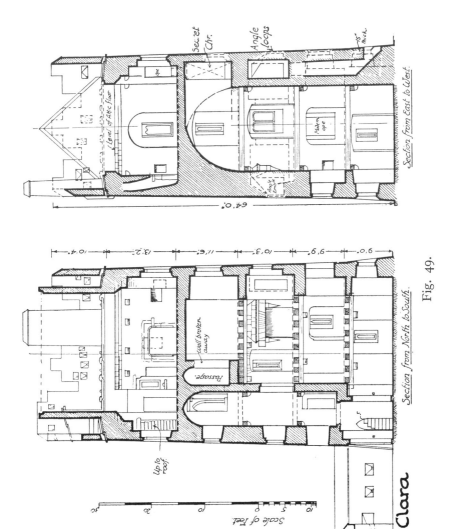

Section from East to West.

Level of Attic floor.

ope

Sec. of Chr.

Angle Loops

Main ope

Angle Loops

15" thick.

64'. 0".

10' 4".

13' 2".

11' 6".

10' 3".

9' 9".

9' 0".

Section from North to South.

Up to roof.

wall broken away.

Passage.

Fig. 49.

Scale of feet.

30

20

10

5

10

Clara

Fig. 50.

Clara Castle, Co. Kilkenny.

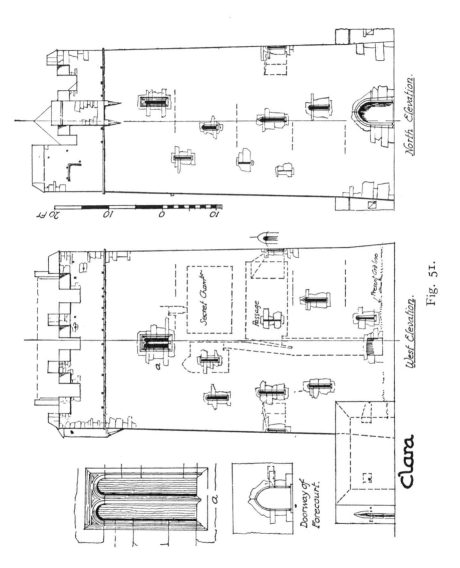

North Elevation.

20 FT.

West Elevation.

Secret Chamber.

Passage.

Prison Cell line.

Clara.

a.

a.

Doorway of Forecourt.

Fig. 51.

But not all of the floors were of timber ; there was, as a
rule one vault of stone—there still is at Clara—barrel shaped
or bluntly pointed, high up in the castle beneath the large
uppermost room.   Often another vault covered the lowest
room or cellar ; frequently this was the only vault in the
building.   In the latest castle houses vaulting was rare.

There is a notable difference in the appearance of the
underside of the vaultings of the XIII century castles of the
Anglo-Normans and those of the later castles of the Irish type.
In the former there are often still to be seen, in the mortar,
the marks of the wooden planking which was used to support
the vault during its construction.   It was the Norman fashion
to use timber for this centreing, as it is called, but the native
builder almost invariably used mats of woven wicker or
basketwork for the purpose.   This was a very simple and,
withal, practical expedient since the mats were easily adjust-
able to any chosen curve and saved quantities of timber.
The impressions of the willow rods—and sometimes even the
rods themselves—are still to be seen in many an Irish castle
vault.   Figure 52 shows the method practised.   Timber
trusses were erected at close intervals and covered with the
wicker work curved to the shape required.   On this surface
there was laid a thick bed of mortar into which the stones of
the arch were set, more mortar being worked in or grouted
from above.   When the whole vault had set quite solidly the
timber trusses were removed but the wickerwork was usually
left in position and, sometimes, plastered over.

The roofs were of high pitch and constructed of timber,
covered with slates, stone slabs, oak shingles, or even thatch.
They were usually gabled ; the gable walls rising from the
inside faces of the walls at the narrower ends of the building
or even slightly inside these walls and carried by rows of
corbels.   The idea, in both cases, was to allow sufficient space
for a narrow alure or wall-walk within the defensive parapet
all round the roof.   Some towers of squarer plan had, however,
hipped, pyramid shaped or conical roofs—similar to those in
the much smaller belfries of the friaries—while others, (there

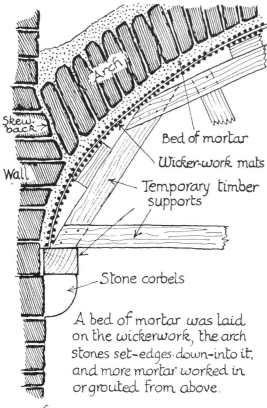

Skew-back →

Wall •

Arch

Bed of mortar

Wicker-work mats

Temporary timber
supports

Stone corbels

A bed of mortar was laid
on the wickerwork, the arch
stones set-edges·down-into it,
and more mortar worked in
or grouted from above.

Vaults built on wickerwork.

Fig. 52.

is a notable example at Termonfeckin in Louth) had a low
conical vaulting of overlapping stone slabs set corbel-wise.
In the ordinary roofs the roof surfaces of slabs, slate or thatch
dripped onto the wall-walk.   This was made of wrought
stone slabs, sloping outwards to drain off the water, and
passing beneath the parapet wall.   Each, or sometimes every
second slab, had an outlet to itself in this wall, while the side
joints between the slabs were covered by saddle-like stones or

cappings.   While the arrangement was sound and effectively
weathertight it had some disadvantages : the alure, obstructed
somewhat by the saddle stones, cannot have been easy or
comfortable to walk on and the slope of the gutter slabs made
the thin walls resting on them rather unstable.   This is one
of the reasons why so many castles lack their parapets to-day ;
they were too easily upset.   The parapets were usually
crenellated in the Irish manner :—the stepped battlement
which appears in Ireland—from where we do not know—in the
fifteenth century.   With their many steps they are very
picturesque ;   excellent examples remain in perfect condition
here and there—particularly in County Wexford, at Clough-
east (Fig. 53), Rathmacknee, Coolhull and other castles, while
the abbey and friary towers, to say nothing of churches,
provide notable examples.   At Clara the parapets are pierced
by nearly thirty small pistol or musket loops but few other
castles show so many examples of a feature which seems to
belong to the sixteenth century, and the succeeding decades.

Fig. 53.

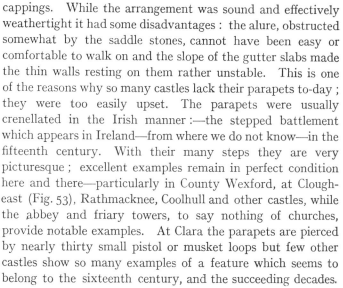

Cloughcast. Wex.
Irish
Crenellations

Another feature of the crowning parapets which may be
seen—but not at Clara—is the means of access to the turret
or turrets which rise above the general level.   These are
usually narrow steps, flags like those of a stone stile, set in
the walls and making very narrow and perilous looking
stairways to the higher parts.

Before leaving the roofs and parapets to discuss the
internal features of our towers another design for or method
of finishing them, sometimes adopted, may be described.
There is a good example of it at BURNCHURCH Castle in
Kilkenny (Fig. 54).   Here the whole of each narrower side
of the castle is carried up a storey higher than the alure as a
sort of wide turret.   In it is a long, narrow chamber or
passage and, above this, a wall-walk with parapets on all
sides.   It is approached by the usual narrow steps set in the
inside face of the turret above the roof slope.   Between the
two turrets was the roof, the turrets serving as gables.

Many, perhaps the majority, of the towers stand isolated
to-day or show but faint traces of surrounding buildings.

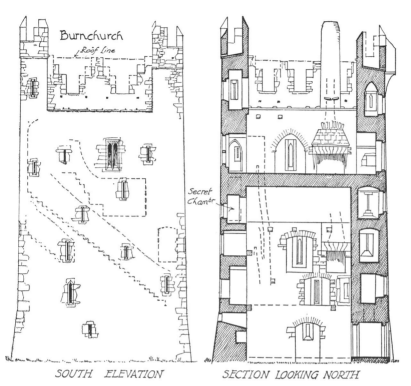

Burnchurch
Roof Line

Secret
Chamᵇʳ

SOUTH ELEVATION   *SECTION LOOKING NORTH*

Fig. 54.

There cannot be much doubt, however, that in most cases
they had been originally enclosed by walled courtyards or
bawns. Some of these are still to be found associated with
certain of the castles. At DERRYHIVENNY (Fig. 55), near
Portumna, in Galway, the greater part of the bawn still
exists. It was L-shaped, as it were embracing the tower and
had two small flanking towers at the extreme opposite corners.
Doubtless both the curtain walls of the bawn and its towers
were crenellated. A gateway, probably protected by a
machicolation, existed close to a one-storeyed building, perhaps
a hall, which occupied the longest side opposite the tower.
At Fiddaun in the same county, a large, six-sided and high-

Derryhivenny Castle, Co.Galway.

D:O'M ME:FIERI:FECIT 1643

Fig 55. Conjectural restoration. Isometric view.

walled bawn surrounds a lofty tower which is isolated in the
centre of the space. Knockelly (Co. Tipperary) also boasts
a very large bawn with angle towers and Carrigafoyle (Co.
Kerry) which stands on the sea shore, had a bawn extending
into the water and enclosing a small dock for boats. The
list might be extended and a careful scrutiny of many a now
isolated tower will often reveal some trace of its one-time
courtyard. The walls of the bawns were, apparently, of no
great thickness or height. Their removal to furnish materials
for modern buildings would be a comparatively easy job ;
they were even more convenient quarries than the high and
more stoutly built towers. The alures on the walls of the
bawns were narrow and were probably extended in width by
the addition of planking on the inside (as seems to have been
the case at Derryhivenny), while the corner towers or low
turrets were often liberally pierced by musket loop-holes. In
a few bawns the gateway remains, set in a narrow building
and guarded by a machicolation impending over the, usually,
round arched opening below.

Some XVIIth century travellers have recorded their
impressions of the Irish castles and the life of the inhabitants.
M. Bouillaye le Gouz, in 1644 says of the Towers :—" The
castles of the nobility consist of four walls ; extremely high
and thatched with straw ; but to tell the truth, they are
nothing but square towers, or at least having such small
apertures as to give no more light than there is in a prison.
They have little furniture, and cover their rooms with rushes,
of which they make their beds in summer, and straw in winter.
They put the rushes a foot deep on their floors and on their
windows, and many of them ornament their ceilings with
branches."

Luke Gernon, in his *A Discourse of Ireland, circa* 1620
(quoted in C. Litton Falkiner's *Illustrations of Irish History*,
pp. 360-1) gives a lively account of hospitality in a castle.
He says : " We are come to the castle already. The castles
are built very strong, and wth narrow stayres, for security.
The hall is the uppermost room, lett us go up, you shall not
come downe agayne till tomorrow. . . . . . The lady of the house

meets you wth. her trayne. . . . Salutations paste, you shall be presented wth. all the drinkes in the house, first the ordinary beare, then aqua vitae, then sacke, then olde-ale, the lady tastes it, you must not refuse it. The fyre is prepared in the middle of the hall, where you may sollace yor. selfe till supper time, you shall not want sacke and tobacco. By this time the table is spread and plentifully furnished wth. variety of meates, but ill cooked and wthout sauce. . . . When you come to yor. chamber, do not expect canopy and curtaines. . . .''

The historian Stanyhurst (in *De Rebus in Hibernia Gestio*, Antwerp, 1584), throws a little more light : '' At their meals they recline, couches being supplied,'' but his further words show that the meal he describes was served in a large hall on the ground level (see note p. 124). Evidently the tables were low.

X

OTHER FEATURES OF THE TOWERS MAINLY INTERNAL.

In Clara Castle there is but one original fireplace, that—very similar to one at BURNCHURCH (Figs. 54 & 56)—in the second storey room. The large room at the top of the building must have been warmed originally by a central fire or brazier resting on the stone floor near its centre ; the smoke from it could only find its way out through an opening or louvre in the roof. At one side of the room is a regular fireplace but this is plainly an insertion since it closes up an original window. A great many of the Irish towers, as originally built, had no regular fireplaces or chimneys. At Carrigaphooca (Co. Cork) for instance, there is no fireplace or flue whatsoever, while in many other examples all the fireplaces, flues and stacks are later insertions made, often, at the sacrifice of one or more windows. The way in which this was done was to build up part of the wide inner embrasure of the window and, literally, quarry out the masonry above for a flue. Where two windows were directly over one another the depth of stonework to be cut through was not great ; moreover, in this case another fireplace was easily provided, the flue from below passing up behind the higher fire. The chimney stacks of these inserted fireplaces were usually built directly upon the alure and obstructed it greatly ; original stacks, however, are often corbelled out somewhat from the walls and do not greatly interrupt the alure.

The fireplaces themselves are wide, as a rule, and spanned by flat arches with " joggled " voussoirs (as at Burnchurch, Fig. 56) bearing against stones at each end called skew-backs. Since the arch is often at some distance from the wall, and bears a heavy sloping hood or " breast " of stone, curved elbow-like stones project from the wall at each side to prevent the skew-backs from spreading to right or left.   Both BURN-CHURCH and COOLHULL (Fig. 56) provide examples. The skew-backs themselves or the stones supporting them from below, die away into the wall as long, straight or curved corbels or, alternatively, rest on upright jambs of stone, as in the early XIVth century fireplace at Ballyloughan (Fig. 58) and in others of later date not illustrated.

In the castles of the late XVth century and onwards the fireplace heads are more often in the form of a more or less flat lintel, curved downwards at each end as in the early XVIIth century example at CASTLEPARK (Fig. 57) and the simpler and later fireplace at DERRYHIVENNY, Co. Galway (Fig. 67)[1] which is of a form very generally used. Where the span is wide the lintel may be in several pieces,

Burnchurch.

Coolhull.

Fig. 56.

[1] See page 104.

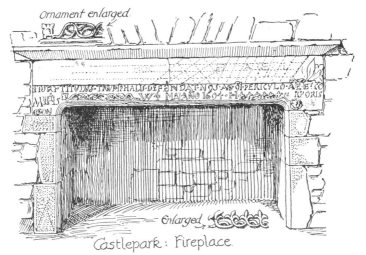

Ornament enlarged.

STVR FTIVLVS IN FIRMALS DEFENDAT NOS AB OMPERICVLO AB E TO
W 4 MAI ANO 1604 H RPORIS
MRHs
GON

Enlarged

Castlepark : Fireplace.

Fig. 57.

Fireplace:
Ballyloughan.
Window : Askeaton.

Fig. 58.

jointed together as were the earlier arches. Its broad surface was a favourite place for the carving of an inscription—often no more than the initials of the builder and his wife or, perhaps, of the mason who made it, as in the Castlepark fireplace—together with a date. Armorials sometimes formed part of the decoration. The flues are large and wide-throated, like those of the traditional cottages still existing in our day. Evidently large fires of wood were the rule.

The typical windows have already been described but there are points about them and the other openings which call for remark. Where the inner embrasures are wide there are often narrow stone seats at each side, as in the fine window of Desmond's XVth century hall at ASKEATON (Fig. 58). The actual openings were commonly closed by wooden shutters, doubtless glazed, fitting against the flat inner parts of the mullions and jambs or into rebates in the stonework. A little search will generally reveal the pivot holes of these shutters worked or bored in the stone of head or sill. Most castles have one or more small openings or loops of which the sill, or a dished stone beneath it, slopes outwards through the wall. These are sink or slop stones.

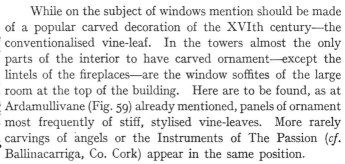

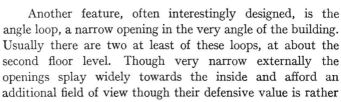

XVIth G. Vine-
Leaf Panel

Fig. 59

While on the subject of windows mention should be made of a popular carved decoration of the XVIth century—the conventionalised vine-leaf. In the towers almost the only parts of the interior to have carved ornament—except the lintels of the fireplaces—are the window soffites of the large room at the top of the building. Here are to be found, as at Ardamullivane (Fig. 59) already mentioned, panels of ornament most frequently of stiff, stylised vine-leaves. More rarely carvings of angels or the Instruments of The Passion (cf. Ballinacarriga, Co. Cork) appear in the same position.

Another feature, often interestingly designed, is the angle loop, a narrow opening in the very angle of the building. Usually there are two at least of these loops, at about the second floor level. Though very narrow externally the openings splay widely towards the inside and afford an additional field of view though their defensive value is rather

doubtful; they could be used for firearms but hardly by a
bowman. The outer opening is most often square at the head
but a round head is also found while some few examples are
very elaborately wrought. That illustrated (Fig. 60), from
COOLE, Offaly, is unique in having had an angle mullion.
A simpler form is illustrated in Fig. 60a[1], together with an
ordinary loop expanded at the bottom for a hand-gun or
other firearm.

In the internal doorways the pointed or round-headed
arch, made up of a few stones, is the most common form, but
square and elliptical heads are also found. Those doors
which lead from the winding stairs or " vice "—such as that
from CARRIGAFOYLE (Fig. 61)—being usually near the
corners of the rooms, have a recess in the room wall beside
them into which the wooden door fitted when it was opened
inwards. No original wooden doors remain to-day but
something of their form may be inferred from the hanging
arrangements still evident. These are, a pivot hole at the
foot—usually wrought in the stone sill—and a sort of hanging-
eye (Fig. 62), also of stone, above it at the top of the same
jamb of the opening. These eyes are rather bulky pieces of
stone, sometimes bevelled and always pierced by a round
hole. Into this the rounded top of the door stile was inserted
and its other end, possibly shod with iron, had its bearing in
the pivot hole below. One example of a hanging eye of wood
remains in position at Derryhivenny Castle, shaped to enclose
the head of the door stile and driven hard into a square hole
in the masonry of the jamb. There are no indications that
the doors had complete frames or even a stile on the closing
side. From the clues it may be inferred that the smaller
doors at least, consisted simply of a timber hanging stile from
which projected two or more rails, and that the upright
planking of the doors was pinned or spiked to the rails. Cross
bolts of wood, sliding back into special holes in the wall when
not in use, seem to have been the usual means of keeping the
doors closed.

The sanitary provisions of the castles, both large and
small, are on the same primitive principle—by flue-like chutes

[1]. See page 98.

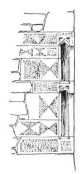

.Plan.

Coole:
Angle Loop &
Ventilators
Fig. 60.

Door from stairs:
Carrigafoyle.
Fig. 61.

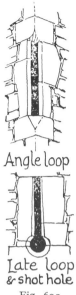

Angle loop

Late loop
& shot hole

Fig. 60a.

Hanging eye

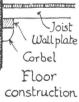

Joist
Wall plate
Corbel
Floor
construction

Fig. 62.

or shafts downwards through the walls from the small mural garderobe chambers on the upper floors, and generally arranged that all the chutes shall deliver together into a common shaft ending near the base of an external wall. In the XIIIth century Roscommon Castle the garderobe chutes—screened by a squinch arch (Fig. 41) in the angles between the corner towers and the curtains—deliver over what was the castle moat or fosse ; in later castles or towers projecting garderobes, though not unknown, are less common than the mural type.

In the towers the machicolation finds a place as a small feature of the parapet, projecting outwards over the entrance doorway many feet below (Fig. 8), or at the more exposed angles of the building. In this position machicolations are sometimes of rounded form, but are often much larger and square, extending along the wall in two directions (cf. Derryhivenny, Fig. 55 and Lisgriffin, Fig. 7). In either case they are borne by well-wrought corbels of stone, between which are the openings for defence. A very favourite form for the corbels is that of long, narrow, inverted pyramids, either straight-sided or slightly incurved (cf. Derryhivenny and Blarney respectively), but shorter, rounded corbels are also found (Fig. 8).

The earlier chimney stacks are simple in form, rectangular or round, slightly tapered and without ornament. By the end of the sixteenth century another type became usual : the picturesque " Jacobean " stack, made up of a number of tubes as it were, set diagonally and connected together in one block. These stacks rise from an oblong base—weathered on the top and often moulded—and are crowned by caps made of narrow, successive projections or of Classic moulded forms, while narrow neck mouldings below the caps are quite usual. Derryhivenny's stacks (Fig. 55) are good examples.

There are few castles which do not possess a secret chamber or strong-box of some kind, though in the later types, where vaults are absent and the walls are relatively thin, the feature is not found. At Clara (Fig. 48) there is a remarkable one at the third storey level between the inner vault and the outside of the wall. Its only entrance, which is on the floor over, is disguised as the seat of a garderobe, and its only opening to the outer air is a mere hole in the wall, hardly visible from the outside. This position in a castle, where there is a great mass of masonry because of the inward coving of the vault, is a favourite place for chambers, more or less secret, which also serve the purpose of reducing the great weight of the structure at this point.

Mural chambers and passages are very common. They lead to or serve as garderobes, ways of access to defensive loops, perhaps sometimes as secret chambers. It is of interest to note that they are usually found on the sides of the tower which look towards the bawn or courtyard, and are therefore less open to attack. The walls towards the " field "—those more subject to direct attack—are seldom weakened by such mural tunnellings.

Fig. 60a is in an outwork of Ballyportry Castle, Clare, later than the castle which itself is hardly earlier than *c*. 1500. It was probably for a hand-gun. Simple oval loops—with the long axis horizontal—are to be found in the bawn wall at Ballyragget, Kilkenny, an erection of the XVIth century. They would suit either hand-guns or muskets.

XI

SOME OTHER TOWERS.

While Clara castle is a good example, both in plan and external appearance, of the smaller towers built in the XVth and XVIth centuries, the form it typifies is not the only one to be found. Not all the variations from the normal can find a place here; the most that can be done is to describe a few of them.

At CARRIGAPHOOCA, Co. Cork (Fig. 63) there is a single tower of broad oblong plan, seated upon the summit of a boss of rock. It is a very simple building with a single apartment in each of its four storeys and has a pointed vault, high within the walls, covering the third storey and supporting the floor of the topmost room which is now roofless. The parapets and gables have gone but it is evident that there were machicolations at two of the corners. A mural staircase of long straight flights gives access to all the floors and the openings seem to have been very simple in form, mere slits or loops. A curious feature of this castle is the entire absence of fireplaces and chimneys, a lack which may indicate a relatively early date in the XVth century or even an earlier period. Another tower in Cork, later and more perfect than Carrigaphooca but very plain, rises starkly from a rocky bluff beside the River Bridge at CONNA, looking like a Rhineland castle in miniature.

RATHMACKNEE Castle, Co. Wexford (Fig. 65), is a very complete and most picturesque small castle built of

Section. thro wall
Carrigaphooca

View.
Carrigaphooca
Fig. 63.

warm-coloured stone. Its tower, nearly square in plan and retaining its crenellations, stands at one corner of a walled courtyard or bawn, entered through a pointed archway over which there is a boldly projecting machicolation. Another, round, machicolation crowns a corner of the bawn.

Also in Co. Wexford is the very attractive COOLHULL (Fig. 66) a late XVIth century castle, which is not a tower but a longish oblong of only two storeys in height, rising in a small narrow tower at one end. Its larger windows are round headed and its crenellations are very complete.

Danganbrack: Roof.

Fig. 64.

Within sight of the well-known friary of Quin, Co. Clare, itself founded upon the ruins of a castle, is DANGANBRACK, a tall tower crowned by high chimneys and four lofty gables (Fig. 64) which, unlike those of many other castles, are flush with the walls. The wall-walks, therefore, are not continuous but occupy only the angles of the tower and expand there into machicolations, two of which are curved in plan. The castle is regarded as one of XVth century foundation but this treatment of the gables belongs rather to the succeeding century; it is probable, indeed, that the top part of the building is actually later than the body of it. Gables of the same kind are found in the castle of LOUGH MASK, Co. Mayo, reputedly built about 1480 but repaired and probably altered in 1618.

While most of the Clare castles are of the simple tower type, there is at least one which presents an interesting variation. It is URLANMORE, situated not far from Newmarket-on-Fergus. It had, and still has a small three storeyed tower at one end and a lower, adjoining extension— apparently of the same date—containing what must have been a fine hall on the upper floor level. In the tower is a small upper room which has outline paintings of animals, etc., on its walls. Even in its partially destroyed state the castle has a remarkable silhouette.

The Clara type persisted in the west well into the XVIIth century, as is evidenced by the very well preserved castle of

Rathmacknee

Fig. 65.

(See also frontispiece).

Coolhull.

Fig. 66.

DERRYHIVENNY, Co. Galway (Fig. 55), erected by Daniel
O'Madden—as the inscription on the corbels of the north-
eastern machicolation tells—in 1643. The illustration, a
conjectural restoration from quite adequate indications and
remains, makes a lengthy description unnecessary. Notable
are the picturesque, diagonally disposed chimney stacks of
Jacobean style and the large angle machicolations of the
alure. The small gabled dormer, which forms the stair head,
and the L-shaped bawn are not usual features though the
round flanking turrets can be found in other castle bawns.
Along one side of the bawn there was a building of one storey
which probably served as a hall for the castle. A door,
windows and a fireplace from Derryhivenny are shown in
Figure 67.

The door " a " is of the pointed form which persisted even
to this late date, its stones are ornamented with picking—less

Derryhivenny Castle ; details.
Fig. 67.

elaborate than those about the loops at Coole (Fig. 60)—while the window " f " is typical in form, square headed and covered by a plain hood-moulding. The small window " c " has a slop-stone, " d " is a ventilator and " e " a loop near the base of the building. The fireplace " b," which has a plain chamfered lintel curved downwards at each end and covered by a chamfered shelf or cornice has already been mentioned (p. 94) as a characteristic type.

A feature, not yet mentioned, of many XVIth and XVIIth century castles in the west and south particularly, is the corner defence jutting out at the second or third floor level. It has no specific name but in effect and intention it is a " bartizan " though not a crowning feature of the corner of the wall. That illustrated (Fig. 68) is at BALLYMALIS

Ballymalis: Wall "Bartizan".

Fig. 68.

castle, Co. Kerry,—a good example and datable to the end of the XVIth century. It is a small, roofed machicolation, with the usual slots between the corbels and several musket loops in the walls. Internally it is a very small L-shaped room, approached by a passage in the corners of one of the upper rooms of the castle.

That a building of one or two storeys, built within the bawn at a little distance from the high tower and containing a spacious hall, was a feature of some at least of the castles is clear from the fragments which remain at several sites. At AUGHNANURE, Co. Galway, a XVIth century stronghold of the O'Flahertys on the shores of Lough Corrib, there still stands in the courtyard one wall of the castle hall. In this wall there are windows, with widely splayed embrasures spanned by wrought stone arches carved in low relief. Vine leaves and other ornaments, almost as elaborate as the enrichments of an early Irish manuscript, decorate the stone work and bear witness to the importance of the building ; many an old house in the City of the Tribes has similar carvings datable to the later part of the XVIth century. Arched window soffits of the same form of construction and decoration are not uncommon ; they are to be found in BALLINA-CARRIGA Castle, Co. Cork, and that at ARDAMULLIVANE in Co. Galway—from which comes the typical vine-leaf carving shown on Fig. 59—and also appear in another castle hall at GRANAGH (popularly Granny) Castle, Co. Kilkenny, where one wall of the hall still stands. The little oriel window (Fig. 69), a seventeenth century addition, is from this castle.

Oriel.
Granagh
Fig. 69.

The little castle of ROCKFLEET (Fig. 70), Co. Mayo, is a neat example of a simple tower of small dimensions. Another small tower is that at BUNCRANA, in Inishowen, Co. Donegal. Its earlier section, because of its very simplicity, is difficult to date with certainty. The fact that the entrance doorway was at the level of the first floor, as in the XIIIth century keeps, suggests an early date, but the parapets, gables, and fireplaces are clearly of much later periods—from 1600 onwards. In plan the tower is oblong, very nearly square,

Rockfleet
Fig. 70.

and in the seven-feet-thick walls are passages and stairways, small chambers and a garderobe, widely embrasured windows and many musketry loops.[1]

In Co. Louth there are numerous towers furnished with one or more turrets of square plan at the angles. These Louth castles seem to be related to the smaller castles of Down, of which Kilclief, and Jordan's Castle, Ardglass, are examples. A good example is that at ROODSTOWN, already briefly mentioned (Fig. 47) which has two turrets, both rising from the ground. One turret holds the winding stairs which leads to all the floors and the roof, while the other contains a garderobe and small chambers. The windows of this castle are particularly good and typical of the XVth century, the period to which this castle belongs. The lights have well-shaped ogee heads with cusps and one (Fig. 71), which has a cross bar or transome and is two lights in width, is a good example of the period. The turrets do not overlap the corners of the building but are extensions, as it were, of the side walls.

Roodstown
Fig. 71.

[1] Davies & Swan : *Ulst. Jour. Arch.* II, pp. 183-188.

Angle turrets too, are sometimes round. At BURT, Co. Donegal, the castle is of late XVIth century date and has these features. The amusing little picture (Fig. 72) of the castle in 1601, and the existing remains, show it to have been a small oblong tower, measuring about 30 feet by 22 feet overall, with two round turrets at its opposite corners (Plan, Fig. 73). One of the turrets contains the staircase. The castle is vaulted within over the main apartment, having gables within the alure in the usual way and seems to have had at least one corner machicolation. Traces of the surrounding bawn with its external ditch—shown with naive particularity in the 1601 drawing, with huts (perhaps temporary quarters for an augmented garrison, or *caponati* cannoneers shelters), large cannon, flanking corner bastions or casemates, besides a gate and bridge—are still discernable on the site to-day. Burt was a seat of the O'Doghertys and was occupied by Docwra in 1601, but returned later to its rightful owners. It was finally captured by government forces in 1608 and remained an important garrison point for a long time.[1]

The square, or rather oblong plan, while the most common, is not the only form ; there are quite a number of castles of round plan. BALLYNAHOW, a Purcell castle in Tipperary, is a good example and there is a quite small tower of similar form at SYNONE (Fig. 74) in the same county. The former has two internal domical vaults, each covering two storeys, while the fifth storey—above the upper vault—was originally covered by a timber roof in the form of a pyramid or cone. The rooms approximate to a square shape and the entrance porch, winding stairs and small chambers are ingeniously planned in one of the thicker segments of the walls. Squinch arches span the corners of the upper storey to carry the pyramidal roof, while high parapets surmounted the walls and three machicolations projected from them. The presence of musket loops beside the principal windows and the general character of the latter suggest a XVIth century date. Synone has very similar arrangements but is altogether on a smaller

[1] Davies & Swan : *Ulst. Jour. Arch.* II, pp. 188-193.

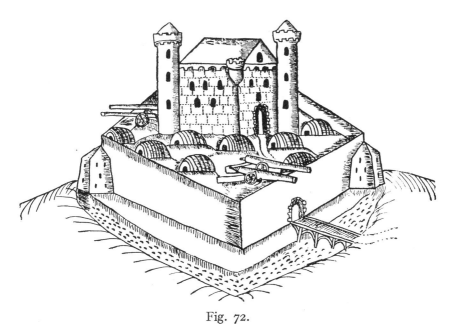

Fig. 72.
Burt Castle, Inishowen in 1601.
(State papers, Ireland, CCVIII, pt. 2, Apl.-May 1601, No. 71v.)

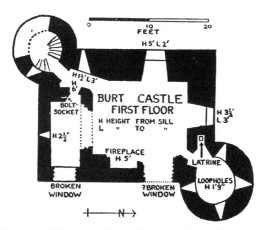

Fig. 73.—Plan of first floor, Burt Castle.

Synone.

Fig. 74.

Reginald's Tower, Waterford

Fig. 76.

Newtown.

Fig. 75.

scale. Another very similar castle is Balief in Co. Kilkenny and the Burren of Clare has some examples also. One of these, NEWTOWN (Fig. 75) is interesting and unusual ; it is nearly round in plan and rises from a square base, the lower walls being in the form of bold spurs. Shot holes, from which the base of the walls could be raked by fire, are ingeniously contrived behind the flat pointed arches at the base of the round part of the building on all four sides. A somewhat similar arrangement occurs in a castle near Castlehaven, Co. Cork, which is, however, square in plan.

A well known round " castle "—it is, in fact, a tower at an angle in the city walls—is REGINALD'S TOWER at Waterford (Fig. 76). If this be the veritable " *turris Reginaldi* " in which, Giraldus Cambrensis tells, the two Syctaracs (Sigtrics) were taken and put to the sword by the Anglo-Normans in the siege and assault of 1170, it has a very respectable antiquity ; indeed, it must be the earliest fortress of mortared stone in Ireland. It is, however, more than possible that the tower we see is a later erection, occupying the site of that of Reginald or Ragnaud the Dane, who, it is claimed, erected his tower in 1003. There is no evidence, so far as the writer is aware, that the Scandinavians—Danes or Norsemen—began to build stone towers and town walls in their own lands so early as the XIth century. Earthen banks and timber palisades seem to have been the customary forms of defensive works. On the other hand, their relatives in Normandy were practised in building more permanent strong works of stone at an even earlier date and the custom may well have found its way to the Ostmen of Waterford. The evidence for the date of Reginald's Tower is inconclusive ; except for its parapets—which were almost certainly of the Irish type but could be additions—it seems to lack features which can be dated with certainty. Quite conceivably it may be no older than the XIIth or XIIIth century at the earliest. This fine remnant appears in Francis Place's meticulous drawing of the city made about 1698[1] much as it is to-day,

---

[1] Maher : *J.R.S.A.I.*, LXIV, p. 52.

but projecting for about half its diameter from the city wall which runs along the Quay. Water extended around the eastern side also (along the present Mall) and a low battery stood out into the Suir at the foot of the tower.

Plate IV

LIMERICK CASTLE
FROM N.W.

WICKERWORK CENTRING

Still in position on undersurface of barrel vault
at Athclare Castle, Co. Louth   (see page 87).

E

XII

THE LARGER CASTLES
OF THE 15TH, 16TH AND 17TH CENTURIES.

The smaller castles, being the most numerous and hitherto the least regarded structures, have been dealt with at considerable length. It remains to consider the less numerous larger castles which are very striking and have more historic associations.

Perhaps the most widely known is the castle of BLARNEY, Co. Cork. Its splendid tower (Fig. 77), some 85 feet in height and given greater impressiveness by its situation, is surely the most frequently photographed Irish building, and is of special interest as being—essentially—a magnification of the lesser towers which are so numerous and characteristic. It was built in two sections ; the first a tall and narrow tower, of no great dimensions, which contains a staircase and smaller rooms ; the second—adjoining and overlapping the earlier work—a massive keep of oblong plan, remarkable for the graceful batter of its walls and the galaxy of Irish battlements which crowns its parapets. These project more than two feet beyond the walls, forming a continuous machicolation, borne by tapering corbels as high as a tall man. A stone in the south face of the older part of the castle is said to bear the inscription :—" Cormac McCarthy Fortis Me Fieri Facit, A.D. 1446."

At the base of the tower the walls are about twelve feet thick and carry a pointed vault (see Fig. 78). Above this the

Blarney Castle, Co. Cork.
crenellations restored.

Fig. 77.

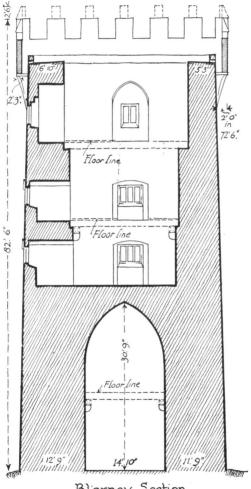

Blarney Section.

Fig. 78.

walls are gradually reduced in thickness in each of the three upper storeys which had timber floors and a timber roof, now gone. Deep, arched embrasures in the walls lead to the windows, which are all square-headed and of two or three lights in width in these rooms.

The castle of Blarney, of which the great keep is but a part, was the stronghold of MacCarthy More, directly descended from the former kings of Desmond. Cormac Laider, or the Strong, who died in 1494, is credited with the erection of the tower, and the stepped Irish form of battlement agrees with his date. The corbels which carry it, however, seem to be of a rather later type of design as also do the larger windows. Conceivably these windows may be insertions and the corbels and battlements a late addition.

There are several other great towers, somewhat less massive than that of Blarney but each possessing special points of interest. Perhaps the finest is that of BUNRATTY, Co. Clare (Figs. 79 and 80), a XVth century erection of the O'Briens of Thomond, which stands beside a small tidal creek of the Shannon estuary, the Bunratty river, between Limerick and Newmarket-on-Fergus. It is an oblong building, lofty, and furnished at each corner with a square tower or turret. A picturesque feature is the broad arch which unites the southern turrets just below the topmost storey and casts a bold shadow on the walls below. The northern face of the building has a similar arch now masked, however, by the brick house inserted between the turrets in the XVIIIth century. On this side is the original entrance doorway, leading into a large vaulted hall in the body of the building. Beneath this hall is a store, also vaulted, and above it is a once magnificent apartment which still retains some of the elaborate stucco work which was its chief ornament in the XVIIth century. While the main block is of three storeys the turrets contain a greater number with small rooms and passages, stairways and chambers too complex to describe. In the south-eastern turret—at the same level as the great upper hall—is a chapel with rich stucco ceiling decorations of *circa* 1619 (Fig. 81).

Bunratty from S.E.

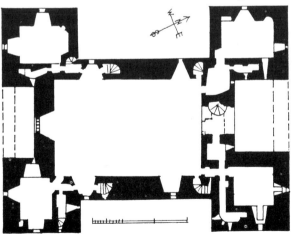

Bunratty: Plan at Upper Hall level

Figs. 79 and 80.

Bunratty: Plaster in Chapel circa 1619

Fig. 81.

Bunratty has had a stirring history, too long for these pages, since de Clare built a stone castle there in 1277. Its predecessor was a bretêsche or wooden tower, erected on a mote in 1251 by Robert de Muscegros. The mote, a small one, is still to be seen but de Clare's stone castle was utterly ruined in the early XIVth century. A new one was built in 1353 by the Justiciar, de Rokeby, but fell to the Irish a few years later, and the present structure is said to have been erected by Maccon MacConmara about 1425. That it has undergone changes in detail during later periods is obvious but, in the main, it is clearly a structure of the prolific later part of the XVth century, and almost certainly to be ascribed to the O'Briens, Earls of Thomond.

At DUNSOGHLY, Co. Dublin (Fig. 82), is another four turreted tower not so massive or unspoiled as Bunratty. Its most interesting feature is the roof of oak (Fig. 83), one of the few original castle roofs of timber still remaining in Ireland. Built in the XVth century by Thomas Plunkett, a chief justice of the King's Bench and a member of a branch of the great Meath family, Dunsoghly is a tall building with gracefully

Dunsoghley

Fig. 82.

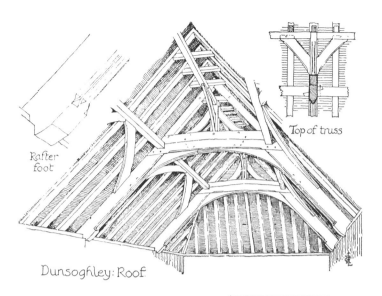

Top of truss

Rafter
foot

Dunsoghley: Roof.

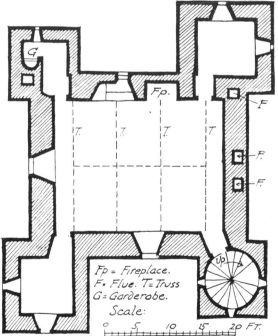

G

Fp.

F

T. T. T. T.

F.

F.

Up

Fp = Fireplace.
F = Flue. T = Truss
G = Garderobe.
Scale:

0   5   10   15   20 FT.

Dunsoghley: Top Floor Plan.

Figs. 83 and 84.

tapering turrets which rise to some height over the parapets of the main block. The lowest of its three storeys is vaulted; but the upper floors were of timber. In the north-eastern turret there is a wide winding stairway of stone while the others contain small rooms. Of these the most peculiar is the prison—the topmost apartment in the south-west turret—only accessible by means of an opening in the bee-hive, corbelled vault above it. The other turrets are also covered in by vaults of the same kind and all have narrow stone stairways leading from the roof-walk to the platforms within the parapets. Close to the south side of the tower is a small detached chapel, built—as the inscription over its neat round-headed doorway proclaims—by John Plunkett, knight, of Dunsoghly, and his wife, Genet Sarsfield, in 1573. An interesting panel, with the Instruments of The Passion, surmounts the inscription. The top floor plan of the castle (Fig. 84), shows the variation in the size of the turrets and how the roof trusses, " T," are arranged. The " prison " is in the smallest turret, over " G."

At a later period, *circa* 1600 to 1640, this castle type, consisting of a main block with turrets or towers at the angles, appears again as a many-gabled house, a development which will be treated of in its place. Other types claim attention first. There are, for example, the large towers placed centrally in walled courtyards. Of these, CARRIGA-FOYLE, Co. Kerry, built between the high and low water marks on the shore near Ballylongford, is remarkable even in its partially destroyed state. The landward half of this tower—80 feet in height and of oblong plan—has fallen away, exposing the section and showing the high, pointed vault beneath its top storey. Patently visible are the small chambers in the haunches of the vault which served to reduce the great weight of this part of the structure and perhaps as secret chambers. Round about the tower there was a strong wall, of which only a small part remains, enclosing—as the XVIth century view in *Pacata Hibernia* shows—not only a courtyard but a dock for boats at the foot of the tower, a feature which must have been unique.

At FIDDAUN, near the Clare border of Co. Galway, is a fine XVIth century castle of the O'Shaughnessys. It is a large, oblong tower of great height, vaulted beneath the topmost storey and standing in the centre of an extensive, six-sided bawn with high and nearly complete walls. There was also a larger outer bawn, not walled but possessing an interesting little gate-building of its own. Before leaving the county of Galway mention must be made of a castle there not so large as Fiddaun and somewhat later in date—DUNGORY, a very complete and attractive building on an islet close to the coast near Kinvarra. It was a place of the O'Heynes, said to have been built in the reign of Henry VIIIth but is obviously later. Standing in the middle of an old dún—its gabled tower rising from one wall of an irregularly shaped six-sided bawn, flanked by a small, square and gabled towerlet—Dungory is a striking little pile.

BALLYGRENNAN, Co. Limerick (Fig. 85) and KNOCKELLY, near Fethard in Tipperary, also have extensive walled bawns and high, centrally placed towers of XVIth century date. There are two of these courtyards at the first named castle, bordered by high gabled and chimneyed houses of later date. At Knockelly the bawn has several low, strong turrets at its corners while the tower itself is unusually high.

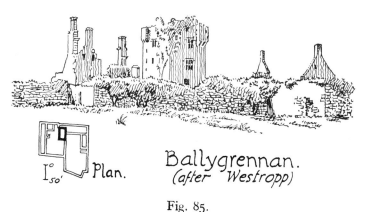

Ballygrennan.
(after Westropp)

Fig. 85.

The largest, mainly XVth century, castle in Ireland is the splendid pile at CAHIR, Co. Tipperary (Fig. 86). It does not fit into any type category and has never—so far as the writer is aware—been thoroughly surveyed or analysed in detail. It has, moreover, been restored in part. Within its high enclosing walls there are several irregularly shaped courtyards, a hall, and a massive keep which dominates a complete and very imposing structure. The strong site at Cahir was occupied by other fortresses many centuries before the castle was built. A fort there was destroyed in the third century and in later times it was one of the residences of Brian of the Tributes. The place is also mentioned in the Brehon Laws.

Cahir Castle

Fig. 86.

It is strange that the Anglo-Normans did not recognize its strategic importance but raised their great mote—probably on a pre-existing Irish earthwork—at Knockgraffon, some miles away. Built in the XVth century, it was said of it, about a hundred years later, that it was " the only famous castle in Ireland that was thought impregnable, and a bulwark of Munster." None the less, Essex had the only important military success of his campaign there when he took Cahir in 1599, after a siege of ten days.

At ASKEATON Castle, Co. Limerick, the greater part of the visible remains belong to the XVth century though the site is that of a castle built some hundreds of years before. This site is peculiar, being a small island encircled by two branches of the River Deel. In the centre of it an outcrop of limestone was scarped into a sort of mote in the XIIIth century and walls were carried round about part of the island. On this rock there now stands a very tall and narrow tower with interesting windows, together with the remnant of a lofty house of XVIth century date. On the western border of the site is a splendid hall built by the earl of Desmond in the XVth century, and raised upon the remnants of an earlier hall. The apartment is a fine one and has several windows of excellent design (Fig. 58) set in embrasures provided with window seats. The traceried window (Fig. 87) now broken and incomplete, was one of the most elaborate in any Irish castle.

Window, XVth Cy. Askeaton.

Fig. 87.

There are no less than two halls in another Limerick castle, NEWCASTLE OCONYL (Newcastle West). One of these is in a building about 80 feet in length, now much sub-divided, the other—known as Desmond's Hall—is complete and perfect and has a vaulted basement. Both halls are datable to the XVth century though some of the windows of the larger hall are of the general forms common at a much earlier period in England. The transomed, ogee-headed and cusped windows of Desmond's Hall show that it belongs to the later years of the century.

Stanyhurst (*De Rebus in Hibernia*) says :

" So these chieftains . . . own castles, strongly constructed, as regards fortification, and mass of stone work, with which are united, by a close connexion, fairly large and spacious halls, constructed of a compound of potter's earth and mud. These are not securely roofed either with quarried slates, or with rough-hewn stones or tiles, but are as a rule thatched with straw from the fields. In these halls they usually take their meals ; they seldom, however, sleep except in the castles, because it is possible for their enemie with great ease to apply to the covering of the halls blazing torches, inflamed by the fanning of the wind, since that kind of stuff takes fire very rapidly."

XIII

THE TOWERED AND GABLED HOUSES
AND THE PLANTATION CASTLES.

The closing years of the XVIth century and the first decades of that following—the Elizabethan and Jacobean periods in England—saw the erection in Ireland of a number of great, many-windowed and gabled houses which, unlike their English contemporaries, retain sufficient defensive features to justify, in some degree, the popular designation of castle. Their windows are neither so numerous, so large or set so low as those of an English " hall " or " court " of the period, while their turrets, well provided with musketry loops, afford the flanking defences still considered necessary.

The most interesting type is that represented in the southern counties by several fine examples. It consists of an oblong central building of three or more storeys, furnished at each of its angles with a square tower of the same height. The central block has a large gable at each end and a number of smaller ones on its longer walls, while each tower has, or had, four gables, one to each face. The whole layout is usually symmetrical, balanced about a central doorway in one of the longer sides, but the many gables and some variations in the size of the windows give a touch of almost Gothic informality to a design which shows the advance of the ideas of the Classic Renaissance.

Perhaps the most perfect, as also the latest, for it is said to have been a quite new building in 1650 when its chatelaine,

Lady Everard, set it on fire on the approach of the Cromwellian army, is BURNTCOURT, Co. Tipperary, (Fig. 88). The building had no less than twenty-six gables topping its lofty, tapering walls, besides several tall chimneys. The larger windows are square headed, of two or more lights in width, divided by transomes and crowned by square-ended hood-mouldings. Between the uppermost windows of the longer sides bold incurved corbels of stone project and were evidently designed to support defensive galleries of timber—survivals of the early hourds and with the same purpose.

The smaller castle of MONKSTOWN, near Cork, built about 1636, is still well preserved and retains its roofs. It is of the same type as Burntcourt but of sturdier proportions and with fewer gables. Unlike Burntcourt, it has stone machicolations at some of its angles. Another of the type, but more ruinous, is to be seen at MOUNTLONG, Co. Cork. Both these buildings have string-courses to each storey, features which are absent at Burntcourt. There are not lacking some examples of about the same date as the foregoing in which the round form of corner turret appears instead of the square. One of these is KILLENURE, Co. Tipperary, of which Austin Cooper drew a sketch in 1793, showing the turrets finishing in small gabled dormers and a single high chimney to each. The main block which the turrets flank has ga! es, six in all, each terminating in a tall and slender chimney stack and the whole makes a picturesque ensemble rather less formal than many-gabled Burntcourt.

Earlier in the century, about 1609, MacDonagh MacCarthy, Lord of Duhallow, built his huge castle at KANTURK, also in Cork, on the same plan, but never carried it to completion. It is recorded that in a fit of rage at the complaints and the accusations that he was building a fortress, made by his suspicious neighbours—English settlers—to the Privy Council of the day, he had the glass tiles made for its roof-covering smashed up and thrown away and the building stopped. It may be assumed that the intention of the designer was to have many gables to the towers and walls,

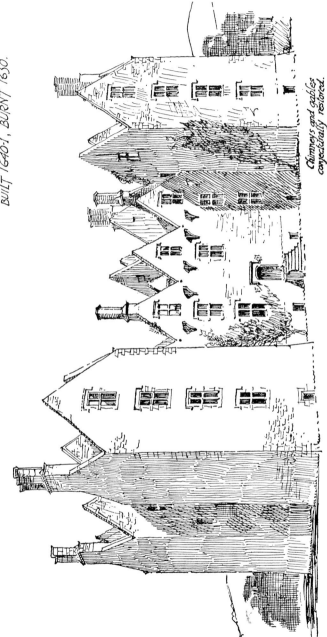

BURNTCOURT CASTLE Cº TIPP.
BUILT 1640-1, BURNT 1650.

Chimneys and gables conjecturally restored.

Fig. 88.

Ea

Kanturk Castle.

Fig. 89.

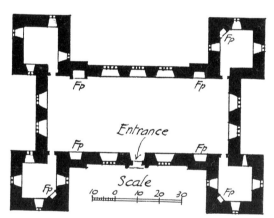

Kanturk: Plan.

Fig. 90.

Plate V

CAHIR CASTLE

ASKEATON : THE XVᵀᴴ CENTURY HALL

rising within the parapets ; the walls, however, stop short at the gutter level and are furnished with rows of very heavy corbels of stone which were to bear the parapets. The entrance is of Jacobean design with pilasters and a bold frieze and cornice about its round-headed doorway. The semi-elliptical arch, however, appears in some of the openings which have hoods of unusual design. The windows are numerous and large in the main block and of smaller size in the wings or towers. See the view and plan (Figs. 89 and 90).

About 1600 at MALLOW, in Cork, Sir Thomas Norreys, or perhaps his daughter Elizabeth, Lady Jephson, raised a castellated house of a somewhat different form to Burntcourt and Kanturk. The precise date is not recorded, but the castle of Mallow—described in detail in a document of 1588—was certainly different in every way to the structure now standing there. Sir T. Norreys died before 1603. The building is a gabled oblong defended at its corners by small turrets of polygonal plan and, centrally, by bold, four-sided projecting wings. In one of these is the entrance, a semi-elliptical headed doorway ; in the other were the stairs and the garderobes. The windows are of the usual type of the times, mullioned and with square heads and hoods. All the floors were of timber, as were also the lintels of the window embrasures, while brick was used in some parts of the walls. The plan is given in Figure 91.

In the south of Ireland at least, the builders of the early part of the XVIIth century seem to have been concerned with providing a house of formal and symmetrical plan, on Renaissance lines, which would none the less be defensible in some degree, witness the flanking turrets of Burntcourt and Mallow and the corbels for a temporary defensive gallery at the former castle. The turreted plan, however, was not the only solution of the problem arrived at ; IGHTERMURRAGH and KILMACLENINE castles, both in Co. Cork, are in the form of a cross, each arm or wing affording flanking protection to the adjacent walls and being liberally provided with shot holes for the purpose. The first named " castle " is a tall

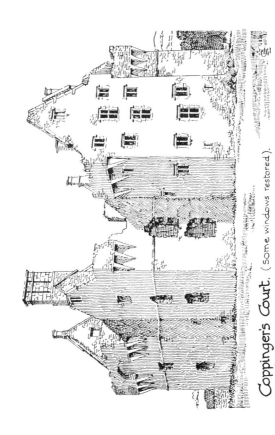

Coppinger's Court. (Some windows restored).

Fig. 92.

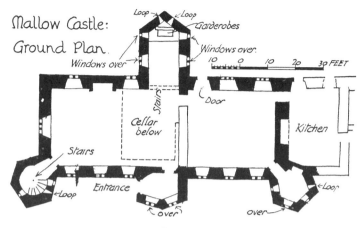

Fig. 91.

building some 60 feet in height to the top of its four gables and seven high chimneys. The interior has many fireplaces, over one of which is an inscription telling that the house was built by Edmund Supple and his wife—" whom love binds in one "—in the year 1641. Kilmaclenine is a smaller and lower building and apparently of about the same date. Yet another form of plan and an even more defensible one is that of the house known as COPPINGER'S COURT (Fig. 92), in the townland of Ballyvireen, near Rosscarbery, in Co. Cork. It consists of an oblong main block with two wings projecting to the front, eastwards—and also slightly to the north and south—while from the centre of its west face there protrudes another wing. The flanking value of all these projections is obvious but the builder was not content with this alone—he provided machicolations at the sides of each wing, features which help to produce one of the most striking buildings of the house-castle type to be found in Ireland. Far less strong in the defensive sense is the smaller castle of GLINSK, in Co. Galway (Fig. 93) which, though provided with small corner machicolations, has no proper flanking defence. It is said to have been built by Sir Ulick Burke, the third baronet of Glinsk, who was included in the Articles of Limerick (1690) and died in 1708. The building seems too early in character for his time and might, with more probability, be ascribed to his predecessor.

The castle of the Purcells at LOUGHMOE, near Temple-more, Co. Tipperary, so well seen from the railway line, is a composite affair ; a XVth century rectangular tower to which is attached a longer and much larger house nearly two hundred years younger. This house has a tower-like wing,

Fig. 93.

rising a storey higher than the main block, and another smaller projection in which is the entrance. Though the house has parapets it can hardly be said to be crenellated—the rising parts finish in small round gables. Each of the storeys is marked by a string-course, while the windows are wide and mullioned and transomed like those of Kanturk. There are many of these windows besides very numerous fireplaces. None of the floors were vaulted and all the interior sub-divisions seem to have been of timber or some other light

Plate VI

LOUGHMOE, FROM THE WEST

LOUGHMOE: INTERIOR OF LATER WING

form of construction. The older tower, on the other hand, has a vaulted ground storey and is also vaulted at a higher level, beneath a large and relatively well lighted room. Each of the narrower end walls is carried up an additional storey and has mural passages, a similar arrangement to Burnchurch. The angles of the tower are rounded. There is a fine fireplace, bearing armorials and initials, in the first floor room and a very curious little chamber—believed to be a prison—high up in the south-east corner of the building and only to be approached from a higher level.

These XVIIth century additions of houses to earlier towers are fairly common; it is not surprising that the inhabitants, with greater security, and advancing ideas of comfort—and becoming tired, perhaps, of mounting steep winding staircases—should call for more spacious and lightsome rooms, arranged more conveniently on a few floors, connected by wide and easy stairs of timber. A good example is to be found at LEMANEAGH, Co. Clare. Here, attached to a tall tower of oblong plan, which has mere slit openings for windows and dates from about 1480, there adjoins on the west side a fine, high-gabled house of four storeys. It is lighted by rows of large mullioned and transomed windows. The ground and first floor storey windows are four lights in width and two in height, divided by transomes. while windows one light less in width light the storey above. The attic rooms have simple three-light windows in the gables. These are peculiar, a full gable in the centre of the front being flanked by two half gables which attain their full height at the corners of the walls. The entrance doorway, which is round-headed, is built-up, as are also the windows of the ground storey. A bartizan is corbelled out of the south-west corner of the building at the second floor level. There was a walled courtyard in front of the castle, entered by an interesting gateway (Fig. 94) which still exists.[1] Its doorway is round-headed, beneath a hood-moulding which is carried up above the arch to enclose two carved shields of armorials and an inscription. The latter gives the names of the builders, Conor O'Brien and his wife, Mary ni Mahon, with the date, 1643. Beside his shield is that

[1] At Dromoland Castle, re-erected in the garden there.

Lemaneagh: Gate.

Fig. 94.

of his son, Sir Donat, who lived about 1690. The double dates
to be inferred are puzzling ; about 1643 would be a reasonable
date, on stylistic grounds, for both house and gateway ;
certainly the general design of the gateway seems too early
for the latter part of the XVIIth century. Evidently the
gateway, and presumably the walls of the courtyard also, had
a projecting defensive parapet, judging by the strong corbels
which still stand out from the top of the stonework.
Lemaneagh was of course a castle of the O'Briens. Here it
was that the tough Mary refused at first to take in the nearly
lifeless body of her husband—wounded in a skirmish with
Ludlow's men—with the words : " We need no dead men
here." To her credit, be it said, she relented and nursed her
man, but unavailingly, for he died the same night. Many a
strange tale is told of fierce Maire Ruadh, most of them
apocryphal ; that she saved the lands for her son by marrying
a Cromwellian cornet of horse seems to be a well-founded
story.

The fine Jacobean wing at DONEGAL castle, which has
so much of the authentic flavour of an English manor house,
is another example of the transformation of a fortress into a
comfortable residence. It is attached to a massive tower built
by the O'Donnells in the XVIth century—if not earlier—and
said to have been burnt by the famous Hugh Roe, before his

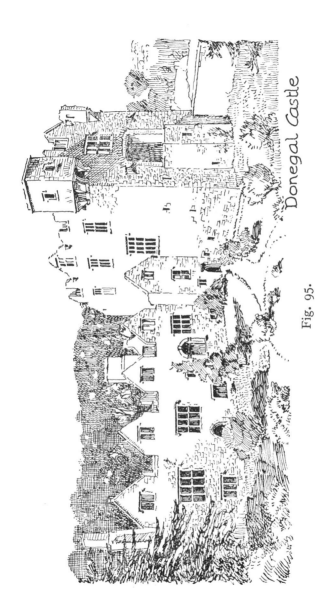

Donegal Castle

Fig. 95.

final departure from Ireland after the battle of Kinsale.   The
lower parts of this O'Donnell tower still remain but the whole
structure was extensively altered by Sir Basil Brooke, the
English grantee.   Mullioned windows of many lights were
made in it—one of them a large bay-window built just over
the position of the original entrance door—and the building
crowned with about a dozen gables.   There remains the whole
of one of the four very heavy square and crude corner turrets
which belong to the same period.   Of the same time is the
ornate Jacobean chimneypiece, ornamented with scrolls,
swags and armorials, which still stands in the main upper room
of the tower, but there are also some fireplaces of an earlier
time and quite Tudor design spanned by four-centred arches.
Figure 95 is a general view looking across the courtyard from
the entrance gateway.

Many of the lesser towers also still show, on one or more of
their walls, the marks where a roof abutted—traces of the
house built in the XVIth century to enlarge the amenities of
the dwelling.   Often all other signs of this house have
disappeared but, in a few cases, the walls remain though in a
broken condition.   Where there are now no such traces the
naive sketches of Thomas Dineley, in his Journal of his
journey through Ireland in the time of Charles II, give
abundant evidence of these houses ; scarcely a castle he draws
but has a more or less elaborate, well-windowed dwelling
beside and joined to it.   The probable reason of the dis-
appearance of so many of these buildings is that they were
more easily worked quarries than the towers for the spoilers
of later times searching for house-building material.   Many
bawn walls suffered the same fate and for the same reason.
Dineley's pictures also show that walled courtyards or rather
fore-courts, laid out in front of and centrally on the axis of the
house or combined house and castle, had become a common
feature by the middle of the century.   The formal and
symmetrical arrangement, characteristic of the ideas of the
Renaissance, had already appeared in the great houses
themselves, as has been said, and was doubtless to be found in
their surrounding features which have disappeared.

The great houses and the additions to castles which have
been cited are evidence that the early part of the XVIIth
century, and especially its fourth decade, were periods of much
building activity in the south of Ireland. In the north—
particularly in the counties of Fermanagh and Tyrone and
between the years 1610 and 1620—another type of defensible
residence was making its appearance. This was the Plantation castle. It had its origin in the parcelling out of large
areas of land—confiscated from the native and rightful
owners—among English and Scotch " undertakers " under
the Jacobean plantation scheme. He who received 2,000
acres had to erect as defensive works a castle and a strong
bawn ; the grantee of 1,500 acres was required to build a house
of stone or brick also provided with a strong bawn, while at
least a bawn was to be made by the lesser man with but
1,000 acres. The planters lost little time in fulfilling the
requirements. Their speed in doing so is not to be wondered
at ; how else could they consolidate their positions in face
of the dispossessed ?

Of the castles and bawns there are many remnants, but
few of them are in any state of completeness. The simplest
type is best illustrated by the well-known bawn of BRACK-
FIELD, Co. Derry. It is a square enclosure, measuring about
70 feet overall in each direction and built of mortared stone.
Two round turrets, disposed at the diagonally opposite angles
to the south-east and north-west, gave flanking defence to the
adjacent sides. Along the inside of the full length of one
wall—the south wall in this case—lay a long house, 20 feet in
width, while another and connected building of the same width
lay at right angles to the house, within and against the west
wall. The rest of the space was an open courtyard about
42 feet square with the main and only entrance in the centre
of its north wall. Some of the bawns were even smaller and
simpler than Brackfield. That at AGHALAHANE, in Fermanagh was but 50 feet square and had (in 1618-19) a wall of clay
and stone and a poor thatched house.

Even the largest of the plantation castles were laid out
on the same general lines as the minor examples—a castle or

strong house filling one side of a more or less extensive bawn which was provided with flanking turrets, round or square, at its angles. The castle or house formed part of the defensive enceinte. In plan it was usually long and narrow, often with a wing or wings projecting into the courtyard, making a T- or L-shaped whole. The turrets of the bawn were usually round and higher than the adjoining walls as in two of the interesting group of castles on the shores of Lough Erne ; CROM and PORTORA. TULLY, another of the same group, has square and oblong flankers at the corners of a bawn measuring about 80 feet in each direction which contains a house of T-shaped plan. The largest bawn is perhaps that of the castle of DUNGIVEN, in Derry. It measures 150 feet by 200 feet and is remarkable in having, within its walls and carried on arches, a wide platform for the defenders.

The most interesting point about the architecture of the houses is the markedly Scottish character given to them by the small round turrets which adorn and defend their upper angles. These features, as in Scottish buildings of the same and earlier periods, are borne by solid rows of corbel courses, strongly moulded (Fig. 96). They were finished—as they still are in the complete and charming " Scots Baronial " house at BALLYGALLEY, Co. Antrim—with little conical, " candle-extinguisher " roofs. At AUGHENTAINE, in Tyrone, there is a considerable fragment of a T-shaped castle which had similar angle turrets as well as a projecting one—for an upper stair-case—carried by a spreading inverted cone of corbel courses of the same design. The roofs of this and of similar castle houses seem to have been of rather steep pitch, with gables to match, while the alure or wall-walk—still common at the same date in the south—does not appear to have been in general use. The turrets, small roofed-in chambers, were quite unlike the open machicolations of Coppingers Court, Glinsk or Monkstown, buildings of slightly later date.

Turret corbels:
Scottish type.
Fig. 96.

Perhaps the most picturesque of all the plantation castles remaining fairly complete is that of MONEA, Co. Fermanagh (Fig. 97). It is an oblong building some 50 feet in height, and

Monea

Fig. 97.

60 feet by 40 feet in length and width. " Scotch " turrets
capped two of its angles while at the other end there still rise
from the ground two more massive rounded towers, flanking
the entrance and crowned in novel fashion—also Scottish—
by rectangular gabled erections. These are carried, in part,
by the typical corbel courses which here serve to develop the
round turret below into the square form above. The " crow-
step " gables of these upper chambers are Scotch, as also are
the simple unmullioned windows. Monea was built by
Malcolm Hamilton, Rector of Devenish, and in 1618-19 still
had its bawn of which but little trace now remains.

The rebellion of 1641 brought most of the plantation
castles to ruin and few of them were ever re-built or restored.

Structures of a very similar type and of about the same
date are to be found outside Ulster and two of them call for
brief mention. One is the castle variously known as PARK'S,
Newtown, or Leitrim Castle, just within the borders of that
county on the shores of Lough Gill. This attractive feature of
the road from Sligo town to Dromahaire village has a large
bawn with two round flanking towers, one of which is a part
of the residence which occupies a corner and about half of one
side of the bawn. It was evidently not considered necessary
to have flankers to the lake shore wall but there is an arched
gate-building of good size adjoining the end of the house.
Another small fortress, the " Castle of the Curlews " at
BALLINAFAD, Co. Sligo, was built about 1610. Its four,
sturdy towers, close set about a small oblong building, recall
the *motif* first seen at Carlow four hundred years before and
repeated at Killenure and other places later. Ballinafad put
up a strong resistance in 1641 and surrendered only for lack
of water.

It was not only the planters who raised defensive
structures in XVIIth century Ulster ; the soldiers played a
part some years before them. Mountjoy built his castle
MOUNTJOY in Tyrone in 1602. This two-storeyed building
of stone and brick is somewhat larger than the County Sligo
building and has turrets square or rather slightly bastion-

shaped in plan. A year earlier the same commander had built a little keep at MOYRY, in Armagh, a simple affair with rounded angles and few features beyond the numerous musket loops. Another work of military character is BENBURB, on a cliff above the Tyrone Blackwater. It has no central and commanding building but consists of a large bawn with liberally loop-holed walls and two rectangular buildings of several storeys which flank the landward extremities. A small round tower stands at another extremity by the cliff edge.

Remarkably like Ballinafad, though smaller and better built, is ROUGHAN, in Tyrone, with its four round turrets and high arch spanning the space between two of them. Unlike the Sligo castle, in which the entrance is in a main wall, the doorway at Roughan is in one of the turrets, Scotch fashion.

(By courtesy of Mr. E. M. Jope, Inspector of Ancient Monuments for Northern Ireland).

XIV

THE FATE OF THE CASTLES.
THE UNDEFENDED HOUSE.

The advent of gunpowder and artillery rang the death
knell of castles. The first fateful bells were, it is true, few
and far separated, since the introduction of siege guns was slow
and the earlier weapons were neither numerous, powerful nor
very accurate. Eventually, however, castle and town wall
went down in rubbish beneath the deadly strokes of the
cannon and great masses of masonry were rent apart and laid
low by a few barrels of gunpowder.

The first mention in the Irish Annals of the use of firearms
of any sort is in the XVth century ; in the year 1487 when,
we are told, an O'Donnell shot an O'Rourke by a bullet from
a gun, presumably an arquebuse, while in the very next year
comes the earliest record of the use of cannon in Ireland ;
at the siege and taking of the castle of Balrath, in Westmeath,
by the Lord Deputy Kildare. It was, of course, the government forces which were best equipped in ordnance ; Essex,
in 1599, besieged and battered Cahir Castle with his heavy
guns and, later still, the siege train of Cromwell's army—the
heaviest guns brought into the country up to that time—
pulverized the stone walls of more than one city. The
defenders of Limerick in the Williamite sieges were to learn
that flying fragments, struck from the city's ancient walls,
were almost as deadly missiles as the cannon balls which broke
and scattered the masonry.

But not every castle suffered the bombardment of artillery—had this been so very few of them would survive at all to-day. Nor were many of them blown to pieces by gunpowder charges ; that munition was too scarce and costly to be expended on the destruction of minor fortresses. It is true that some buildings, like those on the Rock of Dunamase, were systematically ruined and blown into the huge fragments which often remain, fallen but intact, but the 'slighting' of many castles usually took the form of throwing down the parapets from the walls and breeching some part of them so as to make the place indefensible against any ordinary assault. By far the greater number of the castles never felt the blows of Cromwellian or Williamite artillery, their tale of ruin was long drawn out—a story of neglect by owners and spoliation by them or the other quarriers of later times. Most of them are roofless and abandoned and a prey to the clinging ivy, destructive green mantle beloved of the sentimentalist. Some few are to be found lately or even still inhabited, modified perhaps by a succession of owners (such a one is the very picturesque castle of Drimnagh, Co. Dublin, in which work of the XVIth and following centuries is to be seen). Some have been incorporated into a modern residence. More numerous are those castles which an enlightened owner has maintained in fair condition or has at least preserved from active destruction. It is mainly from this group that the Commissioners of Public Works have accepted for State care (under the National Monuments Act, 1930, and previous enactments) representative buildings, large and small, historically and architecturally interesting. Some sixty-six such have been repaired and are permanently maintained or are awaiting repair at the cost of the State, and the number of castles so treated will be added to as time goes on and as opportunities of acquisition arise. In Northern Ireland, under similar legislation, a number of castles are preserved and maintained while others are under the surveillance of the Ministry of Finance and are thus protected against damage and destruction.

Plate VII

TAAFFE'S CASTLE : CARLINGFORD

GREENCASTLE (INISHOWEN)
GATE BUILDING

The fate of a few of the more important and more fortunate castles among those which have been described may be given in some brief paragraphs.

Dublin Castle, as the centre of government for seven centuries, has naturally undergone many changes in the time. Of these the most drastic was its remodelling between about 1690 and the middle of the XVIIIth century. To this period belong most of the buildings which surround, its courtyards to-day and housed, until recent times, the city residence of the Lord Lieutenant and its state apartments, the dwellings of officials of the viceregal court and the headquarters of some of the departments of state. All the features of the original castle which remain—with the exception of the Record Tower and part of the south curtain wall—are hidden behind the masonry and brickwork of the XVIIIth century. There is reason to think that St. Patrick's Hall, the largest room in the castle, occupies the position of the original hall. The little river Poddle, feeder of the moat which lay to the south and east of the fortress, still flows very much on the line of that defence but beneath the ground in channels of modern construction.

Limerick castle, whose towers were truncated and vaulted to bear heavy ordnance, perhaps as early as the XVIIth century, became and remained a military barrack up to quite recent times. Abandoned for that purpose its courtyard has been converted into the site of a municipal housing scheme, while its ancient features, its towers and curtains, are in State care as a national monument. Athlone, so long a fortress, still serves military purposes as a barracks and the great pile of Carrickfergus was similarly used until, in recent years, it became and has been repaired and maintained as an ancient monument under governmental care.

The two large castles of Cahir and Trim are still in private ownership while the remains of Athenry, Carlow, Roscommon and Mallow castles are now national monuments. Similarly preserved for the future are many smaller examples, such as Clara—used as a residence up to about 35 years ago—

Derryhivenny and Dunsoghly, which was the birthplace of the grand-parents of people still living. The list might be extended but the story would become monotonous—for the most part only a reiteration of the tale of ruin.

Castle building may be said to have ceased about 1640 and fortifications of the more modern type—which were developed to meet the growing effectiveness of artillery—began to be built at a somewhat earlier time. These newer works, which have received little study as yet, are not within the scope of this book however military their purpose.

The transition from the embattled house, more or less defensible, to the undefended residence has been dealt with at some length in these pages already, but little has been said about the latter type of building. Such houses began to be built in the early years of the XVIIth century, while defensible houses were still the rule rather than the exception, a fact which justifies some reference to these immediate successors of the castle.

The largest and most attractive house is CARRICK-ON-SUIR (Fig. 98) built in the last years of Queen Elizabeth's reign or early in that of her successor, by Thomas, Earl of Ormonde and Carrick, who died in 1614. It stands in front if a double towered castle erected in the middle of the XVth

Carrick on Suir

Fig. 98.

century. This older building forms and closes one side of a
courtyard which is bounded by the later house on the other
three. There is a tradition that Anne Boleyn, grand-daughter
of a Butler and the ill-starred second wife of Henry VIII,
was born in Carrick. The tradition appears to have little
foundation and could not, in any case, apply to the house,
which was not built before the end of the reign of Elizabeth,
her daughter. The house is long and low compared with the
castle towers which rise beside it. Many attractive gables
with pillar-like finials at base and apex crown its walls ; its
many windows are mullioned and wide, each light rounded at
the head in the fashionable, semi-elliptical, late XVIth
century manner. The whole of the entrance porch, which
has a round-arched door, becomes a bay-window in the upper
storey, matching another of similar form in the eastern wing
of the building. What was the finest room in the interior is a
long gallery on the upper floor, perhaps the only remaining
Irish example of a feature characteristic of the great
Elizabethan and Jacobean houses of England. Up to the year
1909 this apartment, originally of the whole—90 feet—length
of the house, possessed two ornate fireplace mantels. Of these
the largest bears the Butler arms and supporters and a long
inscription and is now in Kilkenny Castle. The only remnants
of the room's rich decoration are stucco wall panels, heraldic
and allegorical.

Though Elizabethan Carrick is practically the contemporary of castles like Mallow and Kanturk it does not seem to
have set a fashion in domestic country house building.
Perhaps few lands had the same peace and security as the
Ormonde domains in this part of Ireland. In the cities,
however, notably in Galway and Kilkenny, there are still to
be seen some houses of the same and somewhat earlier periods
and similar style. Galway has its very remarkable Lynch's
" castle," which preserves in its walls a wonderful collection
of elaborately moulded and carved windows, coats of arms
and other features, all of the XVIth century. In St. Augustine
Street in the same city, there still stands a doorway, dated
1577, with a semi-elliptical head and a bold hood-moulding,

trimmed and adorned with vine-leaf and other carved decorations, some of which give evidence of a revival of the Celtic *motifs* of four hundred and more years before. The windows of the little building in Carlingford, Co. Louth, known as the " Mint," present another example of the same revival. These town houses tell of the rise of a wealthy merchant class within the shelter of the walls, but outside the towns the castle was the normal type of residence for chieftain and gentleman.

'New College House, Youghal, connected by tradition with Sir Walter Raleigh, is another house apparently belonging to the first years of the XVIIth century and still exhibiting the high gables and massive chimneys of its original form. In external appearance it has been greatly modified by windows and other details of much later dates.

The newer Jacobean and Caroline fashion in English domestic architecture, which was to some extent influenced by the brick building of the Low Countries, made a few appearances in Ireland between 1632 and 1639, in the vice-royalty of Thomas Wentworth, " Black Tom," the Earl of Strafford. Probably it was Strafford himself who introduced it in the huge house known to-day as JIGGINSTOWN " Castle," which stands by the roadside at a short distance from Naas in the county of Kildare. It was Strafford's hope that his royal master, Charles I, would be persuaded to visit Ireland and the great house was intended for his entertainment and as a noble country residence for his viceroy. Royalty never entered it and to-day the house stands in ruin. Strafford left Ireland in 1639 to lay his head upon the block before very long and the subsequent history of his palatial house seems to have been one of neglect, decay and active destruction. It still exhibits some features of great interest. In scale it was palatial and it was perhaps the largest single domestic structure raised in Ireland since the walls of the great hall of Tara sank into clay. It was about 380 feet in total frontage, including the square projecting wings which—over 300 feet apart— flanked each end of the central block. The upper walls are of brickwork, for the most part super-excellent in quality and workmanship, rising on a vaulted basement storey walled in stone. The bases of a number of massive chimneys project from the walls. They also are built of brick and have bases of Classic section, built up and moulded in the same material. All the window openings have well-constructed flat arches of brick and were originally filled by timber frames, with mullions and transomes, and, doubtless, leaded glazing in small panes. The most remarkable feature of the building, one still virtually intact, is the groined vaulting of the basement storey. It is entirely in brick and borne by centrally placed rows of stout, panelled and moulded pillars of the same material. Moulded arches and groin ribs of brick span the spaces from column to column and wall, supporting the main vaults above. All this brickwork has a technical perfection not exceeded in any subsequent building in the country.

Jigginstown is one of the very few purely domestic erections of the time of which any considerable and recognizable remnants remain. Another, now more ruinous, is the house at OLDBAWN (Fig. 99), near Tallaght, Co. Dublin, erected during the same brief period, *circa* 1635. Its builder was Archdeacon Bulkeley, of the Welsh family of the name, and son of the then reigning Archbishop of Dublin. His new house was burned in 1641—at the hands of the O'Byrnes and

Fig. 99.
Ⓞlꝺbawn, ᴛallaᵹht.

O'Tooles, it is said—but was re-edified some years later. It was of the typical late Tudor plan, shaped like a letter H, a traditional form then rather out of date in England but still in use in the Wales from which the Bulkeleys came. A hall with a large room over it formed the central bar, while the wings—the uprights of the H—contained on the one side the kitchen and offices and on the other a parlour and other private apartments. In the parlour was a fine mantel-piece (now in the National Museum, Dublin) whose central and dominating feature was a " picture," in modelled plaster, representing the re-building of the walls of Jerusalem as told in the book of Nehemiah—apposite indeed to the position of the worthy archdeacon vis-a-vis the Wicklow clans who had destroyed his first house. Tall armed figures flank the centrepiece and the whole conception, and particularly the use of stucco for pictorial, figure and decorative subjects, are evidence of its origin in Wales where plaster was often put to the same uses. The house was gabled and had tall and massive chimneys ; its windows were of square proportion and its doorway heavily Classic. Round about the gardens, orchards and courtyards of the place was a water-filled moat or fosse, a last relic of the troublous times of its building.

The times were to be rather more than less troubled till the end of the century ; the period which included Drogheda and Wexford, Derry, Aughrim and the Boyne, Limerick's sieges and capitulation, "transplanting" and spoliation, was no time for the building of mansion or pleasure house. The latter half of the XVIIth century is therefore, architecturally speaking, a featureless gap.

To it there succeeded the period of active building which we call Georgian, which was at its highest intensity from about the middle of the XVIIIth century to its end. In it were raised the solid, four-square, symmetrical Classic blocks, which, in the grander examples, had wide-spreading and often colonnaded wings to add to their grandeur. Everything was reasonable, formal and stately if not always architecturally logical. The castle was, indeed, dead ; it had become but a picturesque incident of the demesne, all the more " romantick " if mantled in ivy.

The first stirrings of the Romantic movement, novels of the " Castle of Udolpho " type, and the later, more virile romanticism of Sir Walter Scott, played a part in bringing about a revival of interest in medieval architecture and in the rise of the architectural Gothic Revival. Among its early results were that strange anti-climax, the " castle " of the XIXth century. Ireland provided quite a number of examples in the first part of the century, before the Famine. Anti-climax though it be, this architectural phase cannot wholly be ignored if only for the reason that it affected some buildings of greater antiquity such as the castle of Kilkenny, which had to be provided with doors and windows, battlements and the like in the new fashion. In this particular example the new work is of a higher quality of design than in many others of rather earlier date. Of such potency was this romantic mode that more than one noble or gentleman proposed to clothe his formally planned and symmetrically fenestrated mansion with a gothic and military cloak of the latest antique cut. Some of these gentlemen actually did so with unfortunate effect, others, more sensible, had turreted and embattled piles erected on less formal plans. The design of many of these structures is often good in itself and the construction excellent but the detail is too mathematically precise. Moreover, the incongruity of the many and spacious windows which modern ideas rightly demanded, with the stern and military form of the buildings as a whole, does not appear to have struck either architect or owner. Useless crenellations and dummy loop-holes—often gigantically out of scale—seem to have been the irreducible essential of the style. Here we must leave the Irish castle, its last expression a dummy loop-hole for an impossible bowman : an anti-climax indeed.

The Mote of Dinant
(From the Bayeux Tapestry)

APPENDIX.

THE NUMBER OF CASTLES.

Notes on the number of castles of all types in Ireland, including motes and known sites, together with short lists of some castles of interest which have not been mentioned in the book.

It is to be repeated that no comprehensive survey of the whole country has yet been made. Surveys have, however, been carried out in certain areas, notably Northern Ireland, the counties of Limerick, Clare, Cork and Kerry and the diocese of Ossory. There are also extant XVIth century lists of the castles of several counties. The numbers given below are based on these surveys and lists and—for the unsurveyed areas—on published material and an examination of the Ordnance maps. Since closer research would probably increase the numbers they must be regarded as only minimum approximations.

The total of over 2,900 castles is certainly too small, though it is much greater than the number existing to-day—even in a very shattered state—since it includes many castles occupied in the XVIth century which have more or less completely disappeared. The lists then made, however, do not include castles, and particularly motes which had gone out of use or memory at that time. None the less, taking the surveys made, the Ordnance map indications, historical references and the lists themselves into account, the numbers given below may be taken—in the author's opinion—as fairly accurate indications of the distribution of castles throughout the country.

The following abbreviations are used for some of the sources relied on :

S.N.I.—" *A Preliminary Survey of the Ancient Monuments of Northern Ireland.*"

West.—Papers in *Proceedings of the Royal Irish Academy*, by T. J. Westropp.

O.S.—*Ordnance maps* published by the Ordnance Survey, first edition.

Carr.—*History of the Diocese of Ossory*, by the Rev. W. Carrigan.

U.J.A.—*Ulster Journal of Archæology*, Third Series

ANTRIM, including 27 motes and a number of
      XVIIth century buildings (*S.N.I.*)   ..   48
    Antrim mote.
    Donegore mote.
    Knockaholet mote.
    Dunseverick, mid-XVIth century gatehouse.
    Shane's Castle, several dates.

ARMAGH, including a mote, the remainder being
      mainly of the XVIIth century (*S.N.I.*) ..   9
    Richhill, XVIIth century.

CARLOW, including at least 4 motes (*O.S.*) show   ..   37
    Castlegrace mote, near Ballon.
    Castlemore, near Tullow, mote.
    St. Mullin's   do.
    Clonmore, Hospitallers' castle, XIIIth centy.
    Leighlinbridge, of the Burnchurch type.
    Huntington, Clonegall, XVIIth century,
      modernised.

CAVAN.   On (*O.S.*) there are very few castles
      indicated—only 12 certainly—but several
      townlands bear the prefix castle which
      may indicate the previous existence of a
      fortress or house there   17
    Cloughoughter, a round castle on an islet.
    Kilmore mote.

CLARE.   *West.* describes a number and lists   ..   225
    Ballinalackan, modernised and occupied,
      has a courtyard.

Coolisteague, a XVth century tower, nearly
perfect, built in two parts.

Derryowen, XVth-XVIth century tower.

Dromline, do. do.

Rosslara, XVth century, has unusual vaulting.

CORK. The schedule in the *Journal of the Cork
Historical and Archæological Society*, 1913,
gives 325

Ballincollig, large, said to be *temp.* Edward III.

Barryscourt, rebuilt in 1585, has an
interesting chapel and a fireplace with
inscription.

Belvelly, small XVth-XVIth century tower.

Carrigadrohid, late castle at centre of bridge.

Castle Donovan.

Castlemore, largest of the Cork castles after
Blarney, much ruined and of several
dates.

Drishane, 1436, small square tower.

Dromanneen, large XVIth-XVIIth century
house on rock site beside River Blackwater, near Mallow.

Dundanier, 1476, greatly ruined but very
picturesque.

Glanworth, of early foundation, buildings
later.

Inchiquin, round castle with massive walls.

Kilbolane, late XIIIth century, Liscarroll
type.

Kilcrea, XVth century tower, nearly perfect.

Mashanaglass, XVIth century, with two
remarkable " redans."

Shippool, XVth century.

DERRY, including 2 motes, the remainder mainly
XVIIth century (*S.N.I.*) 11

DONEGAL. (*O.S.* and *U.J.A.*), 17 being in the
peninsula of Inishowen 43

Doe Castle, modernised, stands in a fine
bawn defended by a rock-cut fosse.

Termon Maguire, had four turrets.

DOWN, including 25 motes and 8 XVIIth century
  erections (*S.N.I.*) 54
  Audley's Castle, XVth century tower.
  Dromore mote.
  Dundonald do.
  Killyleagh, partly XIIIth century.
  Kirkiston, XVIIth century, large bawn.
  Narrow Water, tower of XVth century
   form but said to be later.
  Sketrick, XVth century tower, partly
   destroyed.

DUBLIN, including one mote. (*O.S.*) and other
  sources show 41
  Bullock and Dalkey, three castellated
   houses, probably of XVth century.
  Howth, gatehouse, square and crenellated,
   XVth century.
  Knocksedan mote.
  Malahide, occupied and much altered.
  Rathfarnham, Elizabethan, bastion-like
   towers. Much altered in XVIIIth
   century.

FERMANAGH, mainly of the XVIIth century (*S.N.I.*) 17
  Castle Archdale.
  Enniskillen.

GALWAY. *The Journal of the Galway Archæological
  and Historical Society* gives a list dated
  1574 from " The Composicion Booke of
  Conaght." 270
  Cargin, oblong, two-storeyed, possibly
   XIIIth century. It is vaulted in the
   lower storey somewhat similarly to
   Athenry Castle and is of about the
   same size.
  Ballinamantaine or Kiltartan, very ruinous
   and extensive, may belong to the late
   XIIIth century.
  Ballindooly, XVth century tower, nearly
   perfect.
  Ballymore, Laurencetown, tower attached
   to modern house.

Claregalway, XVth century tower, nearly perfect.

Drumharsna, XVIth century. All fire-places insertions.

Merlin, nearly perfect tower.

Oranmore, oblong, very well built, XVth-XVIth century.

Pallas, tower in large and perfect bawn.

Terriland, late house, much ruined.

KERRY. A list in the *Kerry Archæological Magazine* (1909) and other sources give   89

Ballycarbery, XVth century oblong tower.

Killaha, late tower-house.

Listowel, XVth century, with arch between turrets (*cf*. Bunratty).

Rahinane, in a rath which served as a bawn.

Ross, Killarney, fine tower of XVth century with later additions and small court-yard with flankers.

Parkavonear or Aghadoe, round and of uncertain date.

KILDARE. (*O.S.*) and other sources show about ..   138

Athy, "White's," small town castle, modernised.

Carbury, picturesque and late, beside a bailey. The mote is gone.

Cloncurry mote.

Donode mote.

Kilkea, modernised but retaining old work.

Kilteel, gate-tower of a larger castle now destroyed.

Naas mote.

Old Connell mote.

Woodstock, XVth century ?, oblong tower.

KILKENNY. In Ossory, which was almost coter-minous with the county, there were—including a number of motes—(*Carr*.) ..   195

Annaghs, a fine oblong tower, XVth-XVIth century.

Ballybur, XVIth century tower with bartizans.

Ballyragget, do., still roofed, with large and
   perfect bawn.
Clomantagh,   do.   do.
Kells mote.
Kells, " the seven castles "—towers in the
   circuit and buildings of the Abbey.
Listerlin mote.
Moatpark, Ballyragget, mote.
Portnascully do.
Tybroughney do.

LEITRIM. (O.S.)   10
   Duncarbry.
   Dromahaire, late house with an early hall
      beside it.
   Rossclogher.

LEIX (Queen's Co.).   On (O.S.) and older maps there
   are about   50
      Note : Ossory extended into Leix and the
      total number is therefore rather less than
      given above.
   Aghaboe, mote.
   Cullahill,   gabled   tower,   XVth-XVIth
      century.
   Killeshin mote; perhaps de Lacy's original
      castle of Carlow.
   Timahoe mote.

LIMERICK.   In survey by West. there are mentioned   405
   Bourchier's, Lough Gur, fine XVth century
      tower.
   Ballingarry, picturesque narrow tower and
      later buildings.
   Ballyculhane, large courtyard with angle
      towers and unusually high walls.
   Cappagh, late XVth century, a five-storeyed
      tower within two enclosures.
   Clonshire, small manorial castle, tower and
      lower attached wing.
   Fantstown, XVIth century tower with good
      fireplaces and bartizans.
   Garraunboy, mid-XVth century tower in a
      small bawn with turrets at all angles.
   Glenogra, XVth century, has an octagonal
      tower.

Oola, XVIth century, gabled tower with fine chimneys.

LONGFORD, including 2 motes (O.S.) 20
Granard mote, partly natural, had stone walls on its summit.
Lissardowlan mote.

LOUTH, including 16 motes, (O.S.) and other sources indicate 71
Ardee, are now Courthouse, and two others.
Athclare, tower house with probably contemporary lower wing
Barmeath, incorporated in modern house.
Cartown, inscribed fireplace, inhabited.
Castletown (Dundealgan) mote, probably originally an Irish work but altered.
Castletown, well preserved XVth-XVIth century tower.
Louth Hall, house attached, inhabited.
Milltown, round turrets.
Dunmahon, a small late tower with turrets.
Heynstown, round turrets.
Taaffe's, Carlingford, a town castle.
Termonfeckin, XVth century tower with low corbelled vault of stone.
Thomastown (Knock Abbey) tower with XVIII cy. house attached. Inhabited.

MAYO. The number of castles extant is not great but a list dated 1574 mentions .. 136

MEATH. There are at least 8 motes and (O.S.) show The number was probably greater. .. 61
Dardistown, in plan like Dunsoghly, Dublin, with perfect original windows. A later wing (1583) connects with modern house.
Diamor mote-and-bailey.
Athlumney, late gabled house and XVth century tower.
Clonard mote.
Oldcastle mote.
Bective, XVIth century tower built into abbey.
Fennor, XVIIth century house.
Liscarton, XVth century tower with turrets.

MONAGHAN. Including two that are doubtful,
    (*O.S.*) show   6
    Clones mote.
    Mannan   do.   (Donaghmoyne).

OFFALY (King's Co.). With possibly 3 or more motes,
    (*O.S.*) and other sources indicate ,   ..   78
    Ballycowan, XVIth-XVIIth century with
        fine chimney stacks.
    Clonmacnoise, square, XIIIth century, on
        a mote.
    Clonony, picturesque but modernised tower
        in a large walled bawn.
    Drumcullen, Kinnitty, mote.
    Kilcolgan, a Jacobean house-castle.
    Leap, modernised but interesting tower.

ROSCOMMON, including 5 which are doubtful, (*O.S.*)
    show   24

SLIGO, including a mote, (*O.S.*) and other sources
    indicate   33
    Ardtarmon, XVIIth century.
    Castlebaldwin, small, L-shaped, XVIIth
        century house.
    Inishcrone, oblong, XVIIth century, with
        turrets at the angles.
    Moygara, a large, square bawn with a tower.
        Date doubtful but probably XVIth
        century.

TIPPERARY. (*O.S.*) and other sources show at least   250
    Ardfinnan, a round keep.
    Ardmayle mote, a very perfect specimen.
    Ardmayle castle, a XVIIth century house
        much ruined.
    Clonamicklon, a large house and bawn.
    Ballydoyle, XVth-XVIth century tower.
    Barretstown,   do.   do.
    Golden, fragment of a round castle.
    Grallagh, XVIth century tower with
        remains of bawn.
    Knockgraffon, XVIth century castle and
        XVIIth century house near mote
        already mentioned.
    Lackeen, XVIth century tower.

Moycarkey, do., central in large bawn.
Two-mile-borris, a tower with bartizans.
Thurles, two towers, XVth-XVIth century.
Gortmakellis, XVth-XVIth century tower.

TYRONE. The castles, nearly all of the Plantation
    type, number (*S.N.I.*)   19
    Derrywoone (Baronscourt), a XVIIth
      century house.
    Castlecaulfield, XVIIth century house.
    Harry Avery's castle, late XIIIth century ?
    Spur Royal, square tower with triangular
      projections on each face. Occupied.

WATERFORD. Including 5 that are doubtful,
    (*O.S.*) shows   58
    Derrinlaur, four towered.
    Lismore mote.
      do.   parts of the Castle.

WESTMEATH, including at least 10 motes (*O.S.*) and
    other sources show   75
    Ballyloughloe or Mount Temple, mote.
    Ballymore mote.
    Castlelost mote.
    Castletown Geoghegan mote.
    Castletown Delvin, double towers remain.
    Fore mote.
      do.   XVth century towers in abbey.
    Kilbixy mote.
    Killare mote.
    Killeenbrack, late tower with bawn.
    Pass Kilbride mote.
    Rathwire mote.

WEXFORD, including some motes, (*O.S.*) and other
    sources show   135
    Adamstown, XVth century tower.
    Baldwinstown, do. with part of bawn and a
      turret.
    Clonmines, remnants of large castle.
    Danes Castle, small and simple tower.
    Ferrycarrig, a slender tower on a rock beside
      the River Slaney.
    Glasscarrig mote.
    Mountgarrett, an oblong tower, probably
      XVth century.

Newcastle mote.

Rathumney, a small " hall."

Slade, tower with lower oblong wing attached, both crenellated.

Taghmon, plain tower.

WICKLOW.   (*O.S.*) and other sources indicate very few   ..   ..   9 or 10

Arklow, fragment of XIIIth century castle

Hollywood, mote on rock outcrop with traces of masonry.

Newcastle, a natural ridge modelled into a mote-and-bailey   A square tower still stands.

A GLOSSARY OF TERMS

USED BUT NOT ALREADY DEFINED IN THIS BOOK.

Batter. The inward sloping of a wall-face. The stronger inclination at the foot of a wall being called a base-batter or talus.

Casemate. A vaulted, loop-holed chamber projecting into the fosse of a fortification, as at BURT (Fig. 72).

Casement. A moulding surrounding a window light or group of lights, bounding the recess in which the lights are set. *cf.* FERNS (Figs. 33 & 34) and CLARA (Fig. 51).

Chamfer. A bevel or slope made by cutting off the edge of anything right-angled.

Chevron. A V-shaped ornament, superficial or moulded. A succession of chevrons produces the zig-zag effect.

Corbel. A projection of stone jutting out from a wall to support a beam or other stonework.

Classic. Appertaining to the Classic styles of architecture of Greece and Rome or the Renaissance architecture based upon them.

Crow-steps. Or " Corbie steps," the stepped form of gable slope, *cf.* MONEA (Fig. 97). A characteristic Scottish feature derived, probably, from the architecture of the Low Countries.

Fore-building. A building, taking various forms, immediately in front of the elevated main doorway of a XIIIth century keep.

Fore-work. A fortification of earth or stone built in advance of the main works.

Fosse. A ditch or moat, either dry or wet, especially one which has contributed the material from which the fortress it encloses has been constructed.

Garderobe. A latrine or privy.

Groin-rib. A groin is the line in which two vaults running at a right or other angle meet. A groin rib is a narrow arch-rib of brick or stone in this position.

Haunch. The haunch of an arch or vault is the middle part, between the springing and the crown of the arch ; especially the mass of material in this position.

Hood-moulding. A narrow, plain or moulded projecting band of stone over the lintel, or arch of a window or door. It usually bends or returns downwards at the ends of the lintel and bends again outwards and downwards or finishes in a narrow point or a carved ornament. Dripstone and label are other names for the same feature.

Jacobean. The style of architecture prevalent in England in the period of James I (1603-1625).

Jamb. The side of a door, window or other opening.

Joggle. A notching of the voussoirs of an arch or the stones of a lintel to prevent them sliding, *cf.* BURNCHURCH, fireplace arch (Fig. 56).

Lintel. A horizontal stone or beam spanning an opening.

Mullion. An upright between the lights of a window—a window of two lights has one mullion ; of three lights, two mullions and so on.

Mural passage. A passage in the thickness of a wall. Similarly a mural staircase or stairs is one contained in the thickness of a wall.

Murdering hole. An aperture in a floor or vault over a doorway or an entrance lobby or passage, through which the defenders could fire upon assailants who had gained an entrance.

Peel or Pele. A name applied to castles, especially the small towers, in the border lands of England and Scotland.

Perimeter. The circuit, " trace " or boundary of a fortress.

Pilaster. A flat, usually rectangular and not prominent, column-like projection from a wall.

Rebate. A rectangular groove or slot cut along a face or angle, often for the purpose of receiving a door or shutter.

Redan. An angular shaped defensive projection, *cf.* Mashanaglass ; not unlike a casemate.

Renaissance. The architecture of the Classic Renaissance, which spread over Europe from Italy in the XVth century, first reaching these islands in the XVIth century. It is characterized by the use of Classic forms of mouldings and decorations in the place of the medieval Gothic forms. It reached its highest development here in such buildings as the Custom House, Dublin.

Roll-moulding. A moulding of round, nearly circular section.

Scots Baronial. The native style of Scottish building in the XVIth and XVIIth centuries, characterized by " crow-stepped " gables, numerous turrets or " bartizans " with candle-extinguisher roofs, or gabled (*cf.* Monea), windows of vertical rather than broad proportions, and Renaissance ornamental features around windows and especially doorways.

Shell-keep. A stone walled mote ; *i.e.* where a stone wall, or a more or less circular trace, has been substituted for the mote palisade. There are many English examples.

Skewback. The sloping stone from which an arch starts at the jamb of an opening.

Soffite. The under surface of a lintel, an arch, or a vault.

Squinch. An arch, or corbelling, spanning the angle between two wall faces which are at an angle with one another, *cf.* ROSCOMMON (Fig. 41).

Stile. The upright member of a door. The hanging stile is that which is pivoted or hinged ; the other is the slapping stile.

String-course. A narrow, horizontal, plain or moulded course of stone.

Transome. A horizontal member dividing the upper from the lower lights of a window.

Voussoir. Any stone in an arch.

Ward. The courtyard of a castle.

INDEX.

Numerals in heavy type indicate the pages in which will be found the more important and detailed matter regarding individual castles and their features ; ordinary type denotes more general references to them, to names of places, etc., and proper names. Italic numerals refer to pen drawings and Roman type to the Plates.

(Note : Castles mentioned only in the Appendix are not included).